WHSmith

Challenge

English

KS3: Year 8

Age 12–13

Steve Eddy and Najoud Ensaff

Acknowledgements

The Publishers would like to thank the following for permission to reproduce copyright material:

Holes by Louis Sachar, Bloomsbury Publishing, 2000.

Animal Farm by George Orwell, A.M. Heath & Co., 1998.

The Most Dangerous Game by Richard Connell, Kessinger Publishers, 2006.

The Moon of Gomrath by Alan Garner, Collins Voyager, 2002.

Point Blanc by Anthony Horowitz, Walker Books, © 2001. Reproduced by permission of Walker Books Ltd, London SE11 5HJ.

'The Hitchhiker' from *The Wonderful Story of Henry Sugar* by Roald Dahl, published by Jonathan Cape Ltd & Penguin Books. Reprinted by permission of David Higham Associates Limited.

Barnardo's website, www.barnardos.org.uk.

'Night Garden of the Asylum' from *New Collected Poems* by Elizabeth Jennings, Carcanet, 2002. Reprinted by permission of David Higham Associates Limited.

The Opposite of Fate by Amy Tan, HarperPerrenial, 2004.

Dinosaur article from the BBC Prehistoric section of the BBC website, http://www.bbc.co.uk/sn/prehistoric_life/

Save the Children extract, from www.savethechildren.net

Every effort has been made to trace all copyright holders, but if any have been inadvertently overlooked, the Publishers will be pleased to make the necessary arrangements at the first opportunity.

First published 2007
exclusively for WHSmith by
Hodder Education, an Hachette UK Company,
338 Euston Road, London NW1 3BH

Impression number 10   9 8 7 6 5 4
Year 2011
Text © Hodder Education 2007

A CIP record for this book is available from the British Library.

Cover illustration: Sally Newton Illustrations

Typeset by Servis Filmsetting Ltd, Stockport, Cheshire

ISBN 978 0 340 94558 2

Printed and bound in Spain.

Contents

Introduction

This book is part of the *Challenge KS3 English* series and is aimed at Year 8. It has been written by two educational writers and examiners who have, between them, over 30 years' teaching experience.

The series aims to stimulate lower secondary school age children. It includes a range of activities to develop reading and writing skills beyond what would normally be experienced in school lessons. Lessons in English at secondary level follow the National Literacy Framework laid down by the government. However, often because of class sizes and ability range, teachers focus their attentions only on key skills from this framework. This *Challenge* book extends students so that they can experience and enjoy English at a higher level.

Readers are presented with reading and writing tasks that are loosely based on the National Literacy Framework but which seek to enrich students' understanding and experience of English. Each double-page section deals with a separate topic.

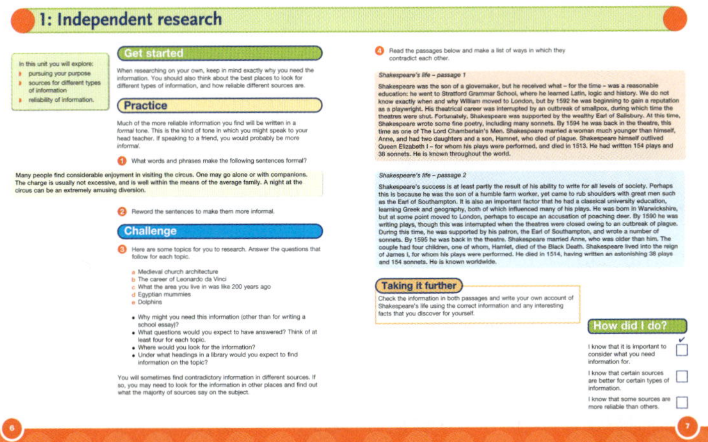

Each unit is divided into digestible subsections of: **Get started**, **Practice**, **Challenge** and **How did I do?**

An introductory box outlines what the focus of the unit will be and the **Get started** section provides more detail about the topic.

The **Practice** section allows students to consider the topic at word or sentence level before the **Challenge** section, which provides students with challenging and interesting extracts that they might not normally encounter in school. The activities aim to stimulate students' imagination and extend their understanding and skills. Where appropriate they are given hints on tasks.

The **Taking it further** boxes suggest extra sources for further research or more demanding tasks. In **How did I do?**, students are encouraged to consider what they have learnt and the skills that they have developed.

A **Glossary** is provided to help students define any difficult words they may come across as they work their way through the book and the **Answers** section gives guidance on possible responses. Fuller answers are provided for the Reading sections but the Writing sections only have answers where these have been practical.

1: Independent research

In this unit you will explore:
- pursuing your purpose
- sources for different types of information
- reliability of information.

Get started

When researching on your own, keep in mind exactly why you need the information. You should also think about the best places to look for different types of information, and how reliable different sources are.

Practice

Much of the more reliable information you find will be written in a *formal* tone. This is the kind of tone in which you might speak to your head teacher. If speaking to a friend, you would probably be more *informal*.

1 What words and phrases make the following sentences formal?

Many people find considerable enjoyment in visiting the circus. One may go alone or with companions. The charge is usually not excessive, and is well within the means of the average family. A night at the circus can be an extremely amusing diversion.

2 Reword the sentences to make them more informal.

Challenge

3 Here are some topics for you to research. Answer the questions that follow for each topic.

   a Medieval church architecture
   b The career of Leonardo da Vinci
   c What the area you live in was like 200 years ago
   d Egyptian mummies
   e Dolphins

- Why might you need this information (other than for writing a school essay)?
- What questions would you expect to have answered? Think of at least four for each topic.
- Where would you look for the information?
- Under what headings in a library would you expect to find information on the topic?

You will sometimes find contradictory information in different sources. If so, you may need to look for the information in other places and find out what the majority of sources say on the subject.

4 Read the passages below and make a list of ways in which they contradict each other.

Shakespeare's life – passage 1

Shakespeare was the son of a glovemaker, but he received what – for the time – was a reasonable education: he went to Stratford Grammar School, where he learned Latin, logic and history. We do not know exactly when and why William moved to London, but by 1592 he was beginning to gain a reputation as a playwright. His theatrical career was interrupted by an outbreak of smallpox, during which time the theatres were shut. Fortunately, Shakespeare was supported by the wealthy Earl of Salisbury. At this time, Shakespeare wrote some fine poetry, including many sonnets. By 1594 he was back in the theatre, this time as one of The Lord Chamberlain's Men. Shakespeare married a woman much younger than himself, Anne, and had two daughters and a son, Hamnet, who died of plague. Shakespeare himself outlived Queen Elizabeth I – for whom his plays were performed, and died in 1513. He had written 154 plays and 38 sonnets. He is known throughout the world.

Shakespeare's life – passage 2

Shakespeare's success is at least partly the result of his ability to write for all levels of society. Perhaps this is because he was the son of a humble farm worker, yet came to rub shoulders with great men such as the Earl of Southampton. It is also an important factor that he had a classical university education, learning Greek and geography, both of which influenced many of his plays. He was born in Warwickshire, but at some point moved to London, perhaps to escape an accusation of poaching deer. By 1590 he was writing plays, though this was interrupted when the theatres were closed owing to an outbreak of plague. During this time, he was supported by his patron, the Earl of Southampton, and wrote a number of sonnets. By 1595 he was back in the theatre. Shakespeare married Anne, who was older than him. The couple had four children, one of whom, Hamlet, died of the Black Death. Shakespeare lived into the reign of James I, for whom his plays were performed. He died in 1514, having written an astonishing 38 plays and 154 sonnets. He is known worldwide.

Taking it further

Check the information in both passages and write your own account of Shakespeare's life using the correct information and any interesting facts that you discover for yourself.

How did I do?

✔

I know that it is important to consider what you need information for. ☐

I know that certain sources are better for certain types of information. ☐

I know that some sources are more reliable than others. ☐

2: Making notes

Get started

You often need to make notes – for example, in order to remember key points from what someone has said, or to summarise information from a book or website so that you can use it in an essay. There are several techniques to use. You also need to make sense of your notes later.

Practice

Abbreviations, *contractions* and *acronyms* are all shortened forms of words or phrases.

- An abbreviation cuts off the end of a word, and sometimes the beginning.
- A contraction takes out the middle of a word.
- An acronym is a word formed of the initials of the most important words in a phrase.

1 Divide the following into the three different types and write down what they all stand for. You may have to research some of them.

BBC	Dr	fridge	WYSIWYG	nimby	Col.	scuba

Challenge

Here are some ways in which you can make notes.

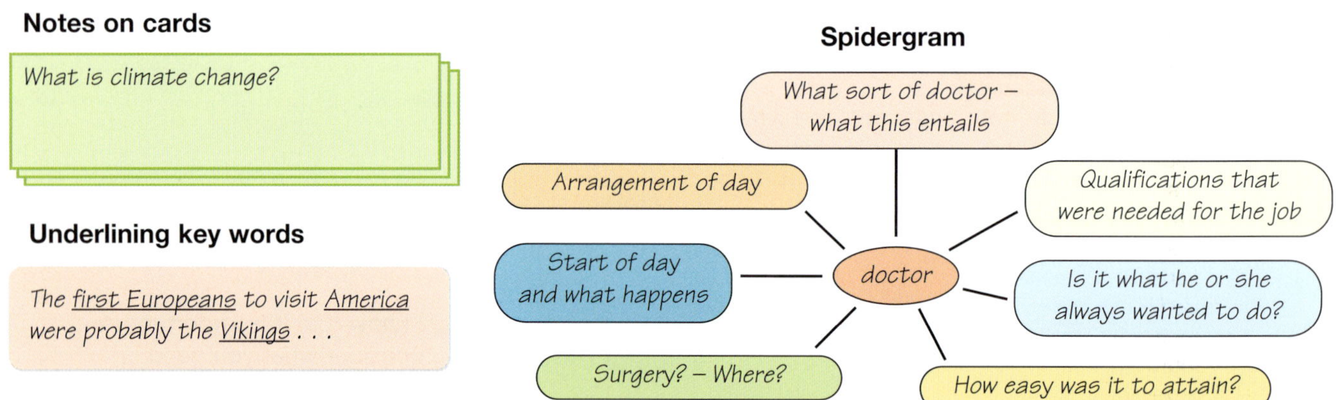

Written linear notes

Climate change. Causes – g/house gases (CO, CO_2), from factories, cars, cows. Effects – rise in temp. but not evenly – Africa hard hit. Also rainfall. Drought. Ice caps melt → flooding, polar bears, etc. Solution: cut unnecessary products, e.g. plastic wrappers = ☺

2 What are the advantages of each method of making notes?

3 Which might you use for each of the following?

    a planning an essay
    b recording the key points of someone else's talk
    c helping you to give your own talk
    d recording key points from a book

4 Write out the notes under the heading 'Written linear notes' (on climate change) as a paragraph, in proper sentences.

5 Use your preferred method to make notes on the following information.

Myths and legends

Myths are very old stories which have changed gradually as they have been passed down by word of mouth, often over thousands of years. No one knows how they began, though some may have started as rituals – for example, acting out a story representing the death of winter and the birth of spring. Legends, strictly speaking, are stories which began with a real event, which was altered in the retelling over a long period of time. In Europe, the best-known myths are Greek – for example, Odysseus being trapped in a cave by the Cyclops, or Theseus killing the Minotaur in the Labyrinth. However, every culture has its myths, and it is interesting that myths worldwide have many similarities, such as the hero being an orphan. Harry Potter is a modern example!

Taking it further

Use one of the methods from this unit to make notes:

- for a talk on what you think the world will be like in 100 years' time
- on a character in a novel you have read.

How did I do?

      ✔

I know that there are several methods for making notes – some better for some purposes than others. ☐

I know that, in notes, I can use abbreviations and not bother with proper sentences. ☐

I know that I must be able to understand my notes. ☐

3: Combining information

Get started

Information comes in many different forms, and even if you are just using two books or two websites, you still need to be able to combine information. In doing this, you need to make sure you do not miss out anything important, but you also need to avoid repetition.

Practice

At sentence level, it is also possible to combine two or more sentences into one single *complex* sentence, using *clauses*.

Example:
Flounders are flatfish. They live at the bottom of the sea. They eat worms. This means that they are carnivores.

becomes

Flounders are flatfish that live at the bottom of the sea and eat worms, which means that they are carnivores.

1 Combine the following into single sentences.

   a Skateboarding started in California. It started in the 1950s. Surfers were trying to surf the streets. It is now popular in many parts of the world.

   b Lacrosse is a game in which players attempt to scoop up a ball and throw it into the opponents' goal. It was invented by Native Americans. They regarded it as good military training.

Challenge

2 Read the two passages that follow and then write one of about the same length or a little longer which combines the most important information from both. You may find that the best way to do this is to note the key points in each passage, then write from your own notes.

a Football is the most popular sport in Britain, as well as being a huge source of income for some. However, it has been around for longer than you may realise. Ball games involving kicking the ball have been played by many cultures for over 2,000 years. They were played in ancient Egypt in 1800BCE. In Egypt the game was linked to fertility rituals to ensure the growth of crops. The Aztecs, in South America, played a ball game which involved kicking the ball, but they were also allowed to hit it and throw it! In North America, a very violent version of the game, called Pasuckaukohowog, was played. The pitch was a mile long and the game went on for days. The early English game, which probably started in the eighth century, was also very violent. Rival villages played, with huge teams, no real rules, and a pitch with no exact boundaries. It was much later, in the 1880s, that proper rules were established and the game began to be taken more seriously.

b The origins of football may go back to ancient China, where, according to some evidence, a similar game was being played as early as 2500BCE. In ancient Egypt, the game was even used as a means of ploughing up the soil for planting! There are records of Native American tribes playing a form of football in the seventeenth century, though they were probably playing it much earlier. Further north, the Inuit played football on ice. One of their myths says that the spirits of the dead play football with the head of a walrus. In England the game was originally a rural pastime. However, it caught on in London, and in 1314 Edward II banned it because of the injuries and damage to property it caused. Even so, it was still popular in Shakespeare's time. In his play *King Lear*, one character insults another by calling him 'a base football player'. At that time, the game was played with pigs' bladders, because they could be inflated. The first football club was started in Sheffield. At one time all the players in a team were local, but in the modern game they may not even be British.

3 Now take your passage and shorten it by including only the most important and interesting bits. Try to cut it down to 100 words.

Taking it further

Choose another topic that interests you and research it online, making notes from at least two websites. Then combine the information into a short essay.

How did I do?

I know that there are many different sources of information. ☐

I know that I need a proper grasp of the information in order to combine information from different sources. ☐

4: Themes

Get started

Themes are the ideas that are explored in a text – for example, the power of love, or the evil of racism. Writers may set out to write about a theme, or it may emerge as they write. Either way, different writers tackle the same theme in different ways.

Practice

Sometimes a theme may be represented by a *symbol* in the text – a thing that broadly represents the idea. For example, hatred could be represented by a gun or a dagger – but these items could also be symbols for other themes.

1 Match the objects below with the themes they might symbolise. Explain your choice.

Symbolic object	Theme
sword	truth
wall	knowledge
unicorn	resistance to oppression
pen	the mystery of the universe
fist	hate
mountains	magic
whale	divided communities

Challenge

Read the passage below, from *Holes* by Louis Sachar, and answer the questions that follow.

'Tell me what you learned yesterday,' said the Warden. 'Surely you can remember that.'

Zero said nothing.

Mr Pendanski laughed. He picked up a shovel and said, 'You might as well try to teach this shovel to read! It's got more brains than Zero.'

'The "at" sound,' said Zero.

'The "at" sound,' repeated the Warden. 'Well then, tell me, what does c - a - t spell?'

Zero glanced around uneasily.

Stanley knew he knew the answer. Zero just didn't like answering questions.

'Cat,' Zero said.

Mr Pendanski clapped his hands. 'Bravo! Bravo! The boy's a genius!'

'F - a - t?' asked the Warden.

Zero thought a moment.

Stanley hadn't taught him the 'f' sound yet.	Zero concentrated hard, then said, 'Chat.'
'Eff,' Zero whispered. 'Eff - at. Fat.'	All the counselors laughed.
'How about h - a - t?' asked the Warden.	'He's a genius, all right!' said Mr Pendanski. 'He's so stupid, he doesn't even know he's stupid.'
Stanley hadn't taught him the 'h' sound either.	

2 What do you think of Mr Pedanski's attitude towards the boy Zero?

3 How does Stanley's attitude compare with this?

4 What theme or themes do you think the author is exploring here?

5 What do you think the author is saying about this theme?

Read the passage below, from *Hard Times* by Charles Dickens, and answer the questions. In the passage a teacher, Mr Gradgrind, is testing the knowledge of a new pupil, Sissy Jupe, whose father trains horses.

Taking it further

Think of novels, plays and poems you have read. Make a list or spidergram of themes that a writer could explore.

'. . . Give me your definition of a horse.'

(Sissy Jupe thrown into the greatest alarm by this demand.)

'Girl number twenty unable to define a horse!' said Mr. Gradgrind, for the general behoof of all the little pitchers. 'Girl number twenty possessed of no facts, in reference to one of the commonest of animals! Some boy's definition of a horse. Bitzer, yours.' . . .

'Bitzer,' said Thomas Gradgrind. 'Your definition of a horse.'

'Quadruped. Graminivorous. Forty teeth, namely twenty-four grinders, four eye-teeth, and twelve incisive. Sheds coat in the spring; in marshy countries, sheds hoofs, too. Hoofs hard, but requiring to be shod with iron. Age known by marks in mouth.'

Thus (and much more) Bitzer.

'Now girl number twenty,' said Mr. Gradgrind. 'You know what a horse is.'

6 What do you think of the way Gradgrind treats Sissy?

7 What theme or themes do you think Dickens is exploring here?

8 What theme do the two passages have in common?

9 What different aspects of this theme are the two authors interested in? (Hint: is Zero really too stupid to learn? Does Sissy really know nothing about horses? Does Bitzer's definition say all there is to know about horses?)

How did I do?

✔

I know that themes are the ideas or topics that an author explores in a text. ☐

I know that writers can explore a theme in different ways, focusing on different aspects of it. ☐

I know that writers explore the themes that have interested people for centuries. ☐

5: Values

Get started

Values are the ideals or beliefs that a writer expresses in a text. Putting it another way, authors express their views on what is important in life, and on morality. They do this either directly, by arguing a case, or through fictional characters.

For example, a non-fiction author might write: 'Honesty is vital in a friendship'; a novelist might write about a character who loses a friend by lying.

Practice

Values can be expressed in action, using the *conditional tense* ('If I were . . . I would . . .').

For example:
If I found £100, I would hand it in.

or

If I found £100, I would spend it – finders keepers, losers weepers!

1. Make up similar sentences to express values based on the following ideals.

   kindness
   loyalty
   justice
   courage
   respect
   perseverance

Challenge

Read the passage below, from a story called 'Strike-Pay', by D. H. Lawrence. Four striking miners have just had some fun riding pit ponies. Then one finds that he has lost his week's strike-pay.

He took off his boots and his stockings. The half-sovereign* was not there. He had not another coin in his possession.
   'Well,' said Chris, 'we mun**go back an' look for it.'
   Back they went, four serious-hearted colliers, and searched the field, but in vain.
   'Well,' said Chris, 'we s'll ha'e ter share wi' thee, that's a'***.'

'I'm willin',' said John Warmby.
'An' me,' said Sam.
'Two bob each,' said Chris.
Ephraim, who was in the depths of despair, shamefully accepted their six shillings.

*half-sovereign – ten shillings   **mun – must   ***that's a – that's all

2 What values do the miners demonstrate?

3 What value does Ephraim show at the end of the passage?

4 Why might miners on strike be especially likely to share in this way?

5 Read the following Shakespeare speeches and, for each speech, answer these questions:

- What values is the character expressing?
- What is the opposite of these values?
- What do you think about these values?

How did I do?

✔

I know that values are beliefs about what matters in life, and how we should behave. ☐

I know that values are based on ideals such as honesty and loyalty. ☐

I know that writers explore values in argument and through characters. ☐

a Falstaff questions whether he should risk death in battle for the sake of honour

Can honour set to a leg*? No. Or an arm? No. Or take away the grief of a wound? No. Honour hath no skill in surgery, then? No. What is honour? A word. What is in that word honour? What is that honour? Air. A trim reckoning! Who hath it? He that died o' Wednesday. Doth he feel it? No. Doth he hear it? No. 'Tis insensible, then. Yea, to the dead. But will it not live with the living? No. Why? Detraction** will not suffer it. Therefore I'll none of it.

*set to a leg – set a broken leg
**Detraction – slander, criticism

(*Henry IV, Part 1*, Act 5, scene 1)

b Siward, an old soldier, learns that his son has died facing the enemy

Why then, God's soldier be he!
Had I as many sons as I have hairs,
I would not wish them to a fairer death:
And so, his knell* is knoll'd.

*knell – funeral bell

(*Macbeth*, Act 5, scene 6)

c Claudio rejects his bride because he thinks she has been unfaithful. Leonato is her father.

There, Leonato, take her back again:
Give not this rotten orange to your friend;
She's but the sign and semblance* of her honour.

*semblance – appearance

(*Much Ado About Nothing*, Act 4, scene 1)

6: Fact, opinion and bias

In this unit you will explore:

- what facts, opinions and bias are
- how writers use all three
- what bias is and how it can be deliberate or accidental.

Get started

Facts are things that are generally accepted to be true and which can be proven.
Example: *Custard contains more calories than cauliflower.*

Opinions are personal viewpoints, which are neither wrong nor right.
Example: *Custard should be banned from school dinner menus.*

Bias is an attitude that makes someone present facts unfairly, encouraging readers to interpret them in one way rather than another.
Example: *Chelsea's heroic play forced a lacklustre Sheffield to a goalless draw*.

Practice

One example of bias in writing is the *ironic* use of quotation marks to tell readers not to take a word or phrase at face value.
Example: *The Minister's 'policy' is actually just a mess of half-formed ideas*.

1 What is implied (suggested) by the quotation marks in the following sentences?

   a I was 'educated' at Cadwallader Comprehensive.
   b My 'home' at the time was a shop doorway.
   c My parents tried to cheer me up with a 'surprise' party.

Challenge

2 Divide the following statements into fact and opinion.

   a A goldfish has a four-second memory span.
   b A goldfish's life is of less value than that of a human.
   c Everest is the highest mountain in the world.
   d Polar bears live in the northern hemisphere.
   e Boys are more intelligent than girls.
   f People used to think that the Sun went round the Earth.

3 Things we think of as facts may one day prove to be wrong. However, this does not make them opinions: they are still factual statements. Match up the half-sentences below to turn them from confused factual statements into correct facts.

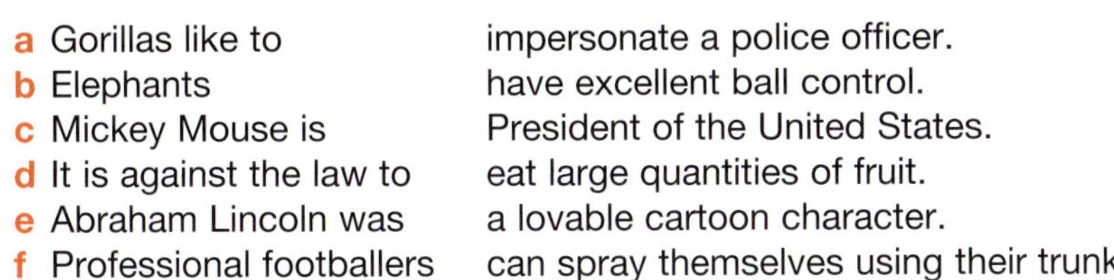

a Gorillas like to	impersonate a police officer.
b Elephants	have excellent ball control.
c Mickey Mouse is	President of the United States.
d It is against the law to	eat large quantities of fruit.
e Abraham Lincoln was	a lovable cartoon character.
f Professional footballers	can spray themselves using their trunks.

4 Read the two newspaper articles below and comment on:

- how they both use the same facts in biased ways
- which article supports the Prime Minister
- which phrases reveal particular bias.

> The Prime Minister today tried to explain away figures showing that street crime is now out of control. Reported muggings have massively increased over the last five years, and there were 2,305 unsolved muggings last month alone. Figures would be worse, but many people now stay at home for fear of muggers, and often do not bother to report crimes.

> The Prime Minister has welcomed figures showing increased public confidence in the police. The public now considers 80 per cent of street crimes worth reporting and arrests have increased. Out of 4,000 street crimes last month – a three-month low – a mere 2,305 remain unsolved. Figures also showed that people now felt more secure in their homes.

5 When you think you have correctly paired the half-sentences in question 3, make up one opinion on each subject.
Example: *We should all adopt an elephant*.

6 Watch two news broadcasts shown on television on the same day but on different channels. Ideally watch one and record another at the same time. Make a table to show:

- what topics each channel covers
- the order of topics and length of time given to each (showing how important each topic is considered to be)
- any possible bias you notice in presentation, such as how someone is described; for example, 'The *confused* Prime Minister stated . . .'.

Taking it further

Buy two newspapers with differing political views, or visit their websites, and see how they have dealt with the same political news story. Identify differences. You could try, for example, comparing the *Guardian* and the *Daily Telegraph*.

How did I do?

I know that facts are generally considered to be true, though they may be wrong. ☐

I know that opinions are viewpoints, and are therefore neither right nor wrong. ☐

I know that bias is a one-sided representation of facts. ☐

7: Irony and satire

In this unit you will explore:
- what irony and satire are
- how writers use them
- how satirical fiction presents a viewpoint.

Get started

Irony is like sarcasm but more subtle. Being sarcastic means sneering at someone or something by saying the opposite of what one really thinks. In Unit 4, Mr Pendanski is being sarcastic when he says 'Bravo! Bravo! The boy's a genius!'. He actually means that the boy is stupid.

Here is an example of writing that is ironic but not sarcastic.

> When I saw the 9.15 express train to Bagshot hurtling towards me, I considered my options carefully. I could write a strongly worded letter of complaint to the appropriate authorities, I could congratulate the driver on his punctuality, or I could finally benefit from my life assurance.

This is ironic because the narrator's careful, formal style is at odds with his situation – and he will not *benefit* much if hit by a train!

Another kind of irony is when something happens that seems particularly inappropriate or unlucky; for example, if someone drives off a cliff when trying to read a road sign like the one below.

Danger: keep your distance!

Satire uses ironic humour to criticise a powerful person, a political system, society or an institution. Novels, plays, poems and TV shows can be satirical.

Practice

The *tone* of a piece of writing reveals the writer's attitude towards the subject and towards readers.

1. Describe the tone of the following sentences and explain how this tone is achieved.

   a Hi, guys! Seems like a million years since we hung out. How's it goin'?
   b We regret to inform you that the company will no longer require your services.
   c While I have the greatest respect for the President, his inability to think and chew gum at the same time could be considered a disadvantage.
   d Garstang at once enfolded the trembling Amelia in his manly arms. 'Oh, Garstang!' she sighed . . .

Challenge

The passage below is from George Orwell's novel *Animal Farm*, which satirises the way in which the ideals of the Russian Revolution were twisted by the new leaders. The leaders are represented by pigs.

All the pigs were in full agreement on this point, even Snowball and Napoleon. Squealer was sent to make the necessary explanations to the others.

'Comrades!' he cried. 'You do not imagine, I hope, that we pigs are doing this in a spirit of selfishness and privilege? Many of us actually dislike milk and apples. I dislike them myself. Our sole object in taking these things is to preserve our health. Milk and apples (this has been proved by Science, comrades) contain substances absolutely necessary to the well-being of a pig. We pigs are brainworkers. The whole management and organisation of this farm depend on us. Day and night we are watching over your welfare. It is for *your* sake that we drink that milk and eat those apples. Do you know what would happen if we pigs failed in our duty? Jones would come back! Yes, Jones would come back! Surely, comrades,' cried Squealer almost pleadingly, skipping from side to side and whisking his tail, 'surely there is no one among you who wants to see Jones come back?'

2 How does the tone of the first paragraph avoid making the criticism too obvious?

3 What proof does Squealer offer that the pigs are not being selfish?

4 How does Squealer use 'Science'?

5 What fear does Squealer use to ensure that the animals are persuaded?

6 How does Orwell make Squealer look ridiculous?

7 How successful do you think this passage is as satire?

8 In *Animal Farm*, the pigs eventually start to do business with the local human farmers – who represent the leaders of non-Communist countries. What do you think is the meaning of the final paragraph (below), in which the animals see the pigs and farmers arguing over a game of cards?

How did I do?

I know that one type of irony is stating the opposite of what one really means. ☐

I know that another type of irony is something happening which seems particularly inappropriate or unlucky. ☐

I know that satire criticises something or someone through humour and ridicule. ☐

Twelve voices were shouting in anger, and they were all alike. No question, now, what had happened to the faces of the pigs. The creatures outside looked from pig to man, and from man to pig, and from pig to man again: but already it was impossible to say which was which.

8: Structure: the shape of a text

In this unit you will explore:

- structure in a text
- the ways in which texts are usually structured
- why authors use structure.

Get started

All texts have a structure, often building up to a climax. A short story often includes a twist or complication. A well structured text leaves the reader with a sense of *resolution*, with mysteries unravelled and tensions relaxed in a satisfying way.

Practice

1 Turn each of the following sentences into shorter ones. The first has been started for you.

a Standing as far forward as I could, and holding the rod away from the trees, I tried to cast my tackle into the centre of the stream, where I might find a fish.
- I stood as far forward as I could.
- I held the rod away from the trees.

b She was beautiful and, more important, she was brave, both of which are desirable features in a trapeze artist.

c Entering the room with an attempt at dignity, I trod on a toy train – abandoned by Ben – and, clownlike, skidded across the floor before landing in a heap.

Challenge

The opening

Read the opening of Richard Connell's short story 'The Most Dangerous Game', and then answer the questions that follow.

'Off there to the right – somewhere – is a large island,' said Whitney. 'It's rather a mystery –'

'What island is it?' Rainsford asked.

'The old charts call it "Ship-Trap Island",' Whitney replied. 'A suggestive name, isn't it? Sailors have a curious dread of the place. I don't know why. Some superstition –'

'Can't see it,' remarked Rainsford, trying to peer through the dank tropical night that was palpable as it pressed its thick warm blackness in upon the yacht.

'You've good eyes,' said Whitney, with a laugh, 'and I've seen you pick off a moose moving in the brown fall bush at four hundred yards, but even you can't see four miles or so through a moonless Caribbean night.'

2 How does the opening arouse our curiosity?

3 What is the men's mood at this point, and how do we know?

4 Why do you think the writer shows the men in this mood?

5 What key facts do we learn?

The development

Rainsford hears shots on the island. Read what happens next and answer the questions that follow.

> He leaped upon the rail and balanced himself there, to get greater elevation; his pipe, striking a rope, was knocked from his mouth. He lunged for it; a short, hoarse cry came from his lips as he realized he had reached too far and had lost his balance. The cry was pinched off short as the blood-warm waters of the Caribbean Sea dosed over his head.

6 How does the mood change, and why?

7 How might the description of the water foreshadow what is to come?

The twist

Rainsford swims to shore and finds his way through the jungle to a house whose owner, General Zaroff, is a keen hunter and a generous host. Over dinner, Zaroff tells Rainsford how he made his hunting more interesting.

> 'I wanted the ideal animal to hunt,' explained the general. 'So I said, "What are the attributes of an ideal quarry?" And the answer was, of course, "It must have courage, cunning, and, above all, it must be able to reason." '
> 'But no animal can reason,' objected Rainsford.
> 'My dear fellow,' said the general, 'there is one that can.'
> 'But you can't mean –' gasped Rainsford.

8 What animal do you think Zaroff might be talking about?

9 What do you think will happen to Rainsford?

The conclusion

The conclusion is given below – all but the last line. Zaroff has dined alone and is going to bed. Guess what has led up to this – and what the final line will reveal.

> 'Rainsford!' screamed the general. 'How in God's name did you get here?'
> 'Swam,' said Rainsford. 'I found it quicker than walking through the jungle.'
> The general sucked in his breath and smiled. 'I congratulate you,' he said. 'You have won the game.'
> Rainsford did not smile. 'I am still a beast at bay,' he said, in a low, hoarse voice. 'Get ready, General Zaroff.'
> The general made one of his deepest bows. 'I see,' he said. 'Splendid! One of us is to furnish a repast for the hounds. The other will sleep in this very excellent bed. On guard, Rainsford.' . . .

Taking it further

Read 'The Most Dangerous Game' online (for example, at www.classicshorts.com) and see if you guessed correctly.

Draw a chart of the structure of the story.

How did I do?

✔

I know that sentences and texts have structure. ☐

I know that stories involve complications, and usually reach a climax and resolution. ☐

9: Comparing texts

Get started

Comparing texts highlights the different style choices the authors have made. This is especially true if the texts have something in common, such as similar themes. Texts can differ in many ways, including subject, theme, viewpoint, imagery and sentence length.

Practice

Texts can be compared on a small scale, at sentence level, as well as on a larger scale.

1 What differences in style do you notice about the following passages?

a I opened the door and entered quietly. There was cigarette smoke in the air. The TV was still on. I caught a glimpse of movement in the mirror opposite. There was someone in the bedroom. I froze.

b I opened the door and crept in to find a thin cloud of cigarette smoke hanging on the air, and the TV flickering. As I glanced around, a movement in the mirror rooted me to the spot.

Challenge

Read Extract **a**, noticing its content and style. Then answer the questions that follow.

a Susan ran from the gate down to the open moor, but she was hardly at the foot of the mountain when there was a shout, and, looking round, she saw another armed man leap over the wall in pursuit.

But was he a man? There was something wrong in the way of his running. He was quick and lizard-dry over the grass: his legs raked forward in pecking strides, and the knee joint seemed to be reversed, while below the knee the leg was thin, and the feet were taloned.

Susan had a fifty-yard lead, but she was climbing while the other was still on the downward slope. She scrambled upwards, trying to keep some energy in reserve, but she was driven by the need for escape.

A spear sighed over her shoulder, and stood out of the ground. This pursuer was not going to risk closer contact. Susan thought to pluck up the spear and use it against its owner, but she could not bring herself to face him, nor to use it, nor even to touch it. So again and again she ran on, renewing her lead while the spear was retrieved, and watching for the next throw.

(Alan Garner, *The Moon of Gomrath*)

2 How does the second paragraph arouse our curiosity?

3 What sort of verbs are used in the extract and what is their effect?

4 Whose viewpoint is the description from?

5 What metaphor is used in the final paragraph and what is its effect?

6 What other features do you notice about the style?

Now read Extract **b**, featuring a boy on a makeshift snowboard, and answer the questions that follow.

b And then he heard the noise coming up behind him. The scream of at least two – maybe more – engines. Alex looked back over his shoulder. For a moment there was nothing. But then he saw them – black flies swimming into his field of vision. There were two of them, heading his way.

Grief's men were riding specially adapted Yamaha Mountain Max snowmobiles equipped with 700cc triple-cylinder engines. The bikes were flying over the snow on their 141-inch tracks, effortlessly moving five times faster than Alex. The 300-watt headlights had already picked him out. Now the men sped towards him, cutting the distance between them with every second that passed.

Alex leapt forward, diving into the next slope. At the same moment, there was a sudden chatter, a series of distant cracks, and the snow leapt up all around him. Grief's men had machine-guns built into their snowmobiles! Alex yelled as he swooped down the mountainside, barely able to control the sheet of metal under his feet. The makeshift binding was tearing at his ankle. The whole thing was vibrating crazily. He couldn't see. He could only keep going, trying to keep his balance, hoping that the way ahead was clear.

(Anthony Horowitz, *Point Blanc*)

7 Compare the two extracts in terms of:

- the use of verbs
- narrative viewpoint
- how the authors bring the passages to life and create a sense of urgency
- use of metaphor (see first paragraph in Extract **b**).

8 Which extract do you prefer, and why?

Taking it further

Write a short essay comparing the two extracts. Try to mention both in each paragraph you write. Include:

- comment on what sort of book you think each extract comes from
- what sort of reader each is aimed at
- your personal response to each.

Reread a few pages from two novels you have read, and then compare their style.

How did I do?

I know that comparing texts is a good way to identify their styles. ✔

I know that fiction can differ in many ways, depending on the author's choices.

10: What is a literary text?

Get started

The author of a literary text wants us to appreciate its style (how it's written) as well as its content (what it's about). Literary texts usually appeal to our imagination, inspire feelings in us, and aim to entertain us.

Practice

In novels, authors often use non-Standard English to make dialogue (speech) more realistic. This could include colloquialisms, local dialect and slang.

1 Turn the following sentences into Standard English.

> **a** She's not short of a few bob.
> **b** I saw some coppers coming so I legged it.
> **c** I polished the knocker and it come up lovely!
> **d** Hang on for a bit and he'll most likely turn up.

Challenge

Literary writers use a number of effects. These include:

- imagery – word pictures that make comparisons
  Example: *. . . a mind like a steel trap*
- appealing to the senses
  Example: *. . . the clatter of pots, the aroma of new bread*
- well chosen words
  Example: *A tormented longing haunted his ravaged features.*
- repetition for emphasis
  Example: *She was bored. Bored with London, bored with Paris, bored with life.*
- varying sentence length
- techniques such as foreshadowing – hinting at what is to come.

Read the passage below, looking out for the effects listed above. Then answer the questions that follow.

Day had broken cold and grey, exceedingly cold and grey, when the man turned aside from the main Yukon trail and climbed the high earth-bank, where a dim and little-travelled trail led eastward through the fat spruce timberland. It was a steep bank, and he paused for breath at the top, excusing the act to himself by looking at his watch. It was nine o'clock. There was no sun nor hint of sun, though there was not a cloud in the sky. It was a clear day, and yet there seemed an intangible pall over the face of things, a subtle gloom that made the day dark, and that was due to the absence of sun. This fact did not worry the man. He was used to the lack of sun. It had been days since he had seen the sun, and he knew that a few more days must pass before that cheerful orb, due south, would just peep above the skyline and dip immediately from view.

(Jack London, 'To Build a Fire')

2 Find two examples of repetition and explain their effect.

3 Find an example of a short sentence followed by a long one.

4 What two senses are involved in the passage? Find one sentence for each sense.

5 What is unusual about the way the trees are described?

6 *Personification* is the description of something as if it were a person with feelings and a personality. Find an example of it in the passage.

7 Find the sentences meaning: 'It wasn't cloudy, but everything looked pale, gloomy and dark in a way you couldn't quite put your finger on, and that was because there was no sun.'
How is Jack London's version more literary?

8 How do you think London wants us to take the line 'This fact did not worry the man'?

9 Read on below and make notes on what makes this extract literary. You might find it helpful to ask yourself what the description would be like if it was meant to be purely factual – like a police report, for example.

How did I do?

	✔
I know that an emphasis on style makes a text literary.	☐
I know that literary features include imagery, repetition for effect, appealing to the senses, and a careful and imaginative choice of words.	☐

The man flung a look back along the way he had come. The Yukon lay a mile wide and hidden under three feet of ice. On top of this ice were as many feet of snow. It was all pure white, rolling in gentle undulations where the ice-jams of the freeze-up had formed. North and south, as far as his eye could see, it was unbroken white, save for a dark hair-line that curved and twisted from around the spruce-covered island to the south, and that curved and twisted away into the north, where it disappeared behind another spruce-covered island. This dark hair-line was the trail – the main trail – that led south five hundred miles to the Chilcoot Pass, Dyea, and salt water; and that led north seventy miles to Dawson, and still on to the north a thousand miles to Nulato, and finally to St Michael on Bering Sea, a thousand miles and half a thousand more.

Taking it further

Find the story ('To Build a Fire' by Jack London) online or in a library.
Read it and look for literary features, especially foreshadowing.

11: What is context?

- what the context of a text is
- social and historical context
- literary context.

Get started

The context of a text means the circumstances that influenced the author and helped to make the text what it is. Social and historical context go together. Society influences the author, and society itself changes over time. For example, Shakespeare's plays reflect the fact that women in his time were expected to stay at home and obey their husbands. The literary context of a text is how the author has been influenced by other writers.

Practice

Words have a historical context – how they have evolved from other words, both in English and in the languages from which English has come.

1. The word-ending *-logy* (as in ornithology, the study of birds) comes from the Greek word *logos* (reason, or knowledge). What words can you think of that end like this?

2. The word-ending *-phobia* (as in claustrophobia, the fear of enclosed spaces) comes from the Greek word *phobos* (fear). What words can you think of that end like this?

Challenge

3. Read the following passages, all published in the nineteenth century. Make notes on what they tell us about nineteenth-century British attitudes towards:
   - poor people
   - children
   - schoolgirls
   - religion
   - exploration
   - foreigners.

a They told me of thousands of beautiful fertile islands that had been formed by a small creature called the coral insect, where summer reigned nearly all the year round, – where the trees were laden with a constant harvest of luxuriant fruit, – where the climate was almost perpetually delightful, – yet where, strange to say, men were wild, bloodthirsty savages, excepting in those favoured isles to which the gospel of our Saviour had been conveyed.

(R.M. Ballantyne, *The Coral Island*, 1858)

b 'Please, sir, I want some more.'

The master was a fat, healthy man; but he turned very pale. He gazed in stupefied astonishment on the small rebel for some seconds, and then clung for support to the copper. The assistants were paralysed with wonder; the boys with fear.

'What!' said the master at length, in a faint voice.

'Please, sir,' replied Oliver, 'I want some more.'

The master aimed a blow at Oliver's head with the ladle; pinioned him in his arms; and shrieked aloud for the beadle.

(Charles Dickens, *Oliver Twist*, 1838)

c 'Humility is a Christian grace, and one peculiarly appropriate to the pupils of Lowood; I, therefore, direct that especial care shall be bestowed on its cultivation amongst them. I have studied how best to mortify in them the worldly sentiment of pride; and, only the other day, I had a pleasing proof of my success. My second daughter, Augusta, went with her mama to visit the school, and on her return she exclaimed: 'Oh, dear papa, how quiet and plain all the girls at Lowood look, with their hair combed behind their ears, and their long pinafores, and those little holland pockets outside their frocks – they are almost like poor people's children!'

(Charlotte Brontë, *Jane Eyre*, 1847)

4 Read the passage below, from Shakespeare's *The Merchant of Venice* (1598).

    a What does it tell us about attitudes to Jews in Shakespeare's time?
    b What do you think Shakespeare's own attitude towards Jews was?

He hath disgraced me, and hindered me half a million; laughed at my losses, mocked at my gains, scorned my nation, thwarted my bargains, cooled my friends, heated mine enemies; and what's his reason? I am a Jew. Hath not a Jew eyes? Hath not a Jew hands, organs, dimensions, senses, affections, passions? Fed with the same food, hurt with the same weapons, subject to the same diseases, healed by the same means, warmed and cooled by the same winter and summer, as a Christian is? If you prick us, do we not bleed? If you tickle us, do we not laugh? If you poison us, do we not die? and if you wrong us, shall we not revenge?

(*The Merchant of Venice*, Act 3, scene 1)

How did I do?

✔

I know that context means the background that influenced the author. ☐

I know that social and historical context reflects changes in society, such as attitudes towards the poor, women and girls, foreigners and ethnic minorities. ☐

12: Genre

In this unit you will explore:
- what genre is
- what different genres there are
- the characteristics of different genres.

A *genre* is a text, usually fictional, with a particular set of features. Some examples are shown below.

comedy   horror   adventure   satire   romance

science fiction   fantasy   crime

Practice

Tenses are important in fiction. Most fiction is in the past tense, but a few novels are written entirely in the present tense.

1. Read the following passage and suggest what the effect is of using the present tense – and the future tense at the end.

I climb the ladder carefully and with my heart beating hard, push open the trap door and manoeuvre myself into the loft. Light filters in through a skylight, dimly illuminating a flurry of dust, which slowly settles as I look around. In the corner stands the chest. What will it contain?

Challenge

2. Read the extracts below. Identify which genre listed under Get started each one falls into.

a Jess hurled herself at the car bonnet and, miraculously, managed to cling to a wiper blade. As the car accelerated she felt its 3 litre engine vibrate beneath her. She grasped the other wiper and braced herself against the sleek metal, lurching sideways as the desperate driver swerved repeatedly in an attempt to dislodge her. Through the windscreen she could see his face, twisted in a mask of fury.

b Varg was no ordinary timelord. He had dominion over an entire fleet of Galactigons. He was not going to let the puny earthlings get the better of him! Making his mind up, he fixed his third eye on the cloudy globe of the Galaxeron, and soon began to experience the familiar sense of lightness that always came when he teleported himself to other planets.

c As the moon slid like a blade from behind the chasing clouds, he caught sight of the child moving fast through the broken gravestones. She was half turned away, but seemed to be shivering. Poor thing, he thought. He lost sight of her for a moment in the shade of an ancient yew tree, and when he saw her again, she was much closer. A chill trickled down his spine. She was standing by a newly dug grave, and as she turned, she smiled. He froze . . .

d Whoever had done this job had been smart – very smart. No fingerprints, not a thing disturbed or out of place. A real pro, thought Stonefield admiringly.

'I want DNA on the wineglass, plus the usual snapshots. Check the answerphone. Maybe our friend made a booking.'

'Guv,' began a nervous PC.

'What is it?' snapped Stonefield, his mind already moving on.

'I think you'd better take a look at this . . .'

3 You probably managed to identify the genres, but can you also list what it is in each extract that gives it away? Look for the less obvious signs as well as the obvious ones. Comment on the tone in each passage, the kinds of verbs and adjectives used, and what sort of details are given.

4 Sometimes two genres can be combined. Which two do you think are used in the following extract?

Spegalon, Overlord of Phlebon, Ultimate Authority on the Third Moon of Betelgeuse, owner of the biggest chain of black holes in the entire galaxy, was having a really bad day. The teleporter had malfunctioned, leaving one of his heads hovering in mid-air several metres above his shoulders. True, two heads are better than one, but only when they are in reasonably close contact. Added to that, he had just accidentally obliterated his own grandmother in a time warp. By rights, he shouldn't even exist.

Taking it further

Think about the last two or three novels you have read. What genres do they most easily fit into, and which features influence your decision?

How did I do?

✔

I know that genres are types of writing with particular characteristics. ☐

I know that many novels fit into a particular genre, such as crime or fantasy. ☐

I know that it is also possible for a novel to combine two genres. ☐

13: Form in poetry

Get started

Form in poetry means how a poem is structured. This consists of two main things:

- *metre* – the number and pattern of syllables in the lines, i.e. the *rhythm*
- *rhyme* – if the poem rhymes, the pattern of rhymes, known as the *rhyme scheme*.

Practice

The smallest pronounceable part of a word is called a *syllable*. A poetic metre consists of a set number of syllables, in a particular pattern of *stressed* and *unstressed*. One bit of this pattern – like one link in a chain – is called a *foot*. Think of it walking along!

Read the following line aloud, counting out the 'beats' of its rhythm:

'If music be the food of love, play on.' (Shakespeare, *Twelfth Night*)

You should find it sounds like this:

De-<u>dum</u>, de-<u>dum</u>, de-<u>dum</u>, de-<u>dum</u>, de-<u>dum</u>.

Each 'de-dum' is a 'foot' of one unstressed syllable followed by one stressed one. There are five pairs.

1. Work out the pattern of stressed and unstressed syllables in the following lines:

   a By the shining Big-Sea-Water
   b O what can ail thee, knight-at-arms
   c Like the leaves of the forest when Summer is green

Challenge

Read the extracts below out loud, beating out their rhythm. Then answer the questions that follow.

Without speaking, without pausing,
Kwasind leaped into the river,
Plunged beneath the bubbling surface,
Through the whirlpools chased the beaver,
Followed him among the islands,
Stayed so long beneath the water,
That his terrified companions

Cried, "Alas! good-by to Kwasind!
We shall never more see Kwasind!"
But he reappeared triumphant,
And upon his shining shoulders
Brought the beaver, dead and dripping,
Brought the King of all the Beavers.

(from Henry Longfellow, 'The Song of Hiawatha')

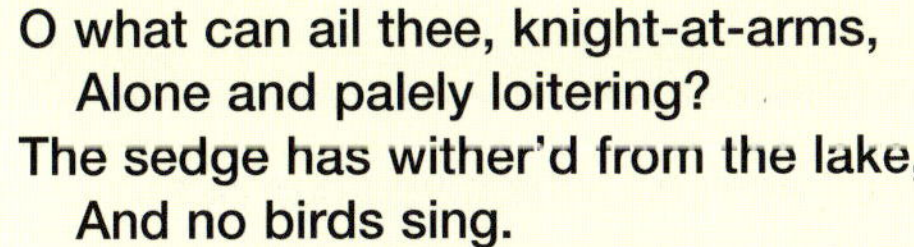

O what can ail thee, knight-at-arms,
  Alone and palely loitering?
The sedge has wither'd from the lake,
  And no birds sing.

O what can ail thee, knight-at-arms!
  So haggard and so woe-begone?
The squirrel's granary is full,
  And the harvest's done.

I see a lily on thy brow
  With anguish moist and fever dew,
And on thy cheeks a fading rose
  Fast withereth too.

(from John Keats, 'La Belle Dame sans Merci')

The Assyrian came down like the wolf on the fold,
And his cohorts were gleaming in purple and gold;
And the sheen of their spears was like stars on the sea,
When the blue wave rolls nightly on deep Galilee.

Like the leaves of the forest when Summer is green,
That host with their banners at sunset were seen:
Like the leaves of the forest when Autumn hath blown,
That host on the morrow lay withered and strown.

For the Angel of Death spread his wings on the blast,
And breathed in the face of the foe as he passed;
And the eyes of the sleepers waxed deadly and chill,
And their hearts but once heaved, and for ever grew still!

(from Lord Byron, 'The Destruction of Sennacherib')

2 How is the rhythm of Longfellow's poem appropriate to its Native American subject?

3 Which poem's rhythm sounds like galloping horses, and why is this appropriate?

4 Which poem has a regular 'ballad' rhythm except for each fourth line – and how does this help to create the mood?

5 Which lines rhyme in Keats's poem?

6 What is the rhyme scheme in Byron's poem and how does it fit the subject?

Some poems are written in an even stricter structure, with a certain number of syllables per line, in a set number of lines.

7 Count the syllables to work out the rules for the following type of poem – a haiku.

The river in flood
Muddy brown water racing
Ducks take a free ride

Taking it further

Search for "Shakespeare" and "sonnet" online. Read one of Shakespeare's sonnets and see if you can work out its form. If you can't work it out, check the Glossary.

How did I do?

✔

I know that the two most important elements of poetic form are rhythm and rhyme. ☐

I know that a set rhythmic pattern is called a metre. ☐

I know that metre and rhyme are used to reinforce meaning. ☐

14: Planning a character analysis

In this unit you will explore:
- how to plan and draft an essay about a character.

Get started

Writers create characters using various devices, which you can use yourself when planning an essay on a character.

Practice

1 Brainstorm some words that occur to you when you think of a rat.

Challenge

Read the following extract from Roald Dahl's short story 'The Hitchhiker'.

Ahead of me I saw a man thumbing a lift. I touched the brake and brought the car to a stop beside him. I always stopped for hitchhikers. I knew just how it used to feel to be standing on the side of a country road watching the cars go by. I hated the drivers for pretending they didn't see me, especially the ones in big cars with three empty seats. The large expensive cars seldom stopped.

It was always the smaller ones that offered you a lift, or the old rusty ones or the ones that were already crammed full of children and the driver would say, 'I think we can squeeze in one more.'

The hitchhiker poked his head through the open window and said, 'Going to London, guv'nor?'

'Yes,' I said. 'Jump in.'

He got in and I drove on. He was a small ratty-faced man with grey teeth. His eyes were dark and quick and clever, like rat's eyes, and his ears were slightly pointed at the top. He had a cloth cap on his head and he was wearing a greyish-coloured jacket with enormous pockets. The grey jacket, together with the quick eyes and the pointed ears, made him look more than anything like some sort of a huge human rat.

'What part of London are you headed for?' I asked him.

'I'm goin' right through London and out the other side,' he said. 'I'm goin' to Epsom, for the races. It's Derby Day today.'

'So it is,' I said. 'I wish I were going with you. I love betting on horses.'

'I never bet on horses,' he said. 'I don't even watch 'em run. That's a stupid silly business.'

'Then why do you go?' I asked.

He didn't seem to like that question. His little ratty face went absolutely blank and he sat there staring straight ahead at the road, saying nothing.

2 Why does the narrator stop for the hitchhiker?

3 What does this suggest about the narrator's character?

4 Identify any words or phrases from the text that tell us about the hitchhiker's character. Look at what he looks like, what he says, how he speaks and what he does. Also look at what the narrator thinks about him.

5 Draw a table like the one below and fill it in, making deductions about what the information in the passage shows us about the hitchhiker.

Quotation from the text	What this shows
'Going to London, guv'nor?'	The man is probably a Cockney.

When you write an essay about a character or any piece of literature, you write what is called a critical essay. A critical essay is made up of three sections: an introduction, a main body and a conclusion.

6 Match the definitions below with each of these sections.

a This section is made up of several paragraphs, each making a point, providing evidence and following on from the previous paragraph.

b This section comes at the start of the essay and is made up of one paragraph, which focuses your essay and gives an idea of its main points.

c This section comes at the end of the essay and is usually one paragraph, which ties up the essay and includes your final comments about the topic.

7 You are going to write an essay answering the question: 'What impression do we gain of the hitchhiker from this passage?'

a Start by organising your ideas about the hitchhiker and deciding which will go in your first paragraph and so on. Think carefully about how you will organise these.

b Write the first paragraph.

c Now, write the next few paragraphs with evidence to support your comments.

d Now write your final paragraph.

This is your draft of the essay. You must now go back and check it for errors in facts, spelling, punctuation and grammar. You should also try to use the best possible English, so reread the essay and try to improve your language.

15: Planning a PowerPoint presentation

Get started

Charities exist to help people in need. They are non-profit organisations that produce informative and persuasive literature to highlight the plight of people and to gain financial support from the public.

Charity websites will give you ideas for creating PowerPoint presentations, which use a combination of words, images and animation.

Practice

1. List some charities that you know of.

2. Read the following passage. Identify which words are emotive and appeal to readers' sympathies.

> Thousands of people die each year from something as simple as poor water supply. Water – something many of us take for granted. Little Joshu is only three years old. Each day his mother Angelie boils water from a river two miles away to allow him and his four sisters and brothers to drink.

Find the Barnardo's website: www.barnardos.org.uk.

Challenge

3 How does the charity make the information on this page easy to understand?

4 How does Barnardo's make this page personal and believable?

5 What is Barnardo's slogan? It appears twice on this page.

6 Which sentences:

> **a** make direct reference to the work Barnardo's has done
> **b** directly address readers?

7 Write down the different ways that Barnardo's offers to help.

8 You are now going to create an informative and persuasive PowerPoint presentation for a charity.

> **a** Research various charities and the sorts of people they represent.
> **b** Think about how you will organise your slides. Decide what you will include on each slide. Have a minimum of five slides. You might organise your slides to include the following:
>
> - charity name, logo and slogan
> - what the charity does
> - some things you didn't know (facts and figures)
> - true story
> - what people can do to help.
>
> **c** Once you have organised your slides, find some relevant information by researching on the internet and in the library.
> **d** Then decide on the slide layout and design. Will you use a standard design or find an image to put as a background?
> **e** Will you include images on any of the slides?
> **f** Consider how your choice of colours and font will reflect your chosen charity.
> **g** Decide on how each slide will move to the next and decide on any animations.

Taking it further

Design a leaflet to accompany your PowerPoint presentation.

How did I do?

✔

I know that a charity might produce a slide show on PowerPoint to inform people about the charity and persuade them to support it. ☐

I know that planning a PowerPoint presentation involves researching the content and thinking about how to organise and design the slides. ☐

16: Parody party

Get started

A parody is an imitation of something that results in it sometimes becoming humorous and exaggerated. A parody of a fairy tale might set the story in a future world or in modern times or might change it in some other way.

Practice

1 List some well-known fairy tales.

2 How do fairy tales traditionally start and what features do they include?

Challenge

Read the following two sections taken from tales.

Long, long ago, in the winter-time, when the snowflakes were falling like little white feathers from the sky, a beautiful queen sat beside her window, which was framed in black ebony, and stitched. As she worked, she looked sometimes at the falling snow, and so it happened that she pricked her finger with her needle, so that three drops of blood fell upon the snow.

It just so happened that on a frosty morning in December Lady Marbury was sitting at her window, reading her copy of *OK!* magazine and watching the snow drift softly down from the sky. She was so preoccupied with watching the snow and flicking through her magazine so energetically that she gave herself a nasty paper cut. Three ruby red drops of blood fell onto a page and all over a football star's face.

3 Which is a parody and which is an original?

4 Which words and phrases helped you decide which story was an original and which was a parody?

Read the beginning of this well-known fairy tale.

Once upon a time there lived a young girl whose father had remarried after her mother's death. This poor girl, named Cinderella, was treated like a slave by her nasty and wicked stepmother, who praised and loved her two blood daughters. She and they would order Cinderella around.

'Get me this. Do that.'

And nothing was ever good enough. They were always criticising Cinderella and making her sad so that one morning she found herself crying in a corner, when there was a knock at the door.

'Who could this be?' Cinderella thought as she walked towards it. Her lazy stepsisters and stepmother were still in bed and it was part of her household duties to sweep and clean, so as she approached the door her face was covered in dust.

> 'Hello,' said a messenger, who was grandly dressed. 'I have an invitation here for this house to attend a ball at the royal palace.' He handed Cinderella the invitation and turned to leave.
>
> 'A ball,' thought Cinderella, her heart brightening with glee. Little did she know that her wicked stepfamily had no intention of letting her go to any ball, or anywhere for that matter.

5 Write bullet points to summarise the remaining plot.

6 Which of the following devices could be used by writers to create humour?

- exaggeration
- long sentences
- understatement
- situations that seem ridiculous
- short sentences
- word play
- stating the obvious
- detail

Read the beginning of a parody of this tale, in which the Cinderella story is told in modern times.

> Once there was a young girl who lived on the outskirts of London with her stepmother, Marsha, her two stepsisters, Sharon and Tracy, and her father, Doug. Cindy was beautiful and clever. In fact, she was hoping one day to become a solicitor and because of this her stepfamily envied her in every way possible. Sharon and Tracy, despite being ugly in look and character, spent each Saturday at the shops buying Gucci handbags and shoes and looking for rich city bankers to trap. They would poke their long and hairy noses into every nook and cranny they could find in the vain hope that they might come across a tall, dark and handsome, but very stupid, rich man who would marry them. Cindy, on the other hand, had to stay indoors washing their clothes and cleaning the house before sneaking in a couple of hours of reading. It was on one such Saturday that Cindy heard a knock at the door.

7 In what ways is this story a parody?

8 Identify words and phrases that give the tale some humour.

9 Look back at your list of bullet points. Continue this parody or create your own.

Taking it further

Read one or two examples of politically correct fairy tales. (Search for "politically correct fairy tale" to find some on the internet.)

Try to write your own version of such a tale.

How did I do?

I know that fairy tales are stories for children, which often involve magic. ☐

I know that a parody uses elements from an original tale and changes these so that they may become humorous, exaggerated, modernised or politically correct. ☐

17: Hauntings

Get started

Poems can be written in a structured way using a set rhythm and rhyme or they can be written in free verse.

Practice

1 What does the word 'haunting' mean? Use a dictionary to check that you are right.

2 Which of the following words and phrases are haunting?

a desk	a dusty mirror
a forgotten tune playing itself on a piano	a distant cry
an old shoe	a computer screen
the turning pages of a book	an envelope
a window banging	a lamp

Challenge

Read the following extract taken from *The Yellow Wallpaper* by Charlotte Perkins Gilman. The narrator in the story suffers from depression; she becomes obsessed with the wallpaper in her room and starts to imagine things.

When the sun shoots in through the east window – I always watch for that first long, straight ray – it changes so quickly that I never can quite believe it.

That is why I watch it always.

By moonlight – the moon shines in all night when there is a moon – I wouldn't know it was the same paper.

At night in any kind of light, in twilight, candlelight, lamplight, and worst of all by moonlight, it becomes bars! The outside pattern I mean, and the woman behind it is as plain as can be.

I didn't realise for a long time what the thing was that showed behind, that dim sub-pattern, but now I am quite sure it is a woman.

By daylight she is subdued, quiet. I fancy it is the pattern that keeps her so still. It is so puzzling. It keeps me quiet by the hour.

3 A haunting atmosphere creates a sense of fear. Which words and phrases suggest the haunting thoughts the narrator in this passage experiences?

4 Sometimes it is what we cannot explain or do not understand that is most haunting. Make a list of inexplicable things that people might find haunting.

Read the following poem, 'Night Garden of the Asylum' by Elizabeth Jennings.

An owl's call scrapes the stillness.
Curtains are barriers and behind them
The beds settle into neat rows.
Soon they'll be ruffled.

The garden knows nothing of illness.
Only it knows of the slow gleam
Of stars, the moon's distilling; it knows
Why the beds and lawns are levelled.

Then all is broken from its fullness.
A human cry cuts across a dream.
A wild hand squeezes an open rose.
We are in witchcraft, bedevilled.

5 This poem is about mental illness. The atmosphere the poet creates is haunting. Identify words and phrases in the poem that have a haunting effect and explain how they create this effect.

6 Look at the sounds of the words in the poem and identify any alliteration or onomatopoeia.

7 Look at the final words in each line in each stanza. Is there any pattern between stanzas?

8 There are several examples in the poem of things being treated in a non-literal way. Jennings uses a number of metaphors. Identify these.

9 You are now going to prepare to write your own poem entitled 'Hauntings'.

   a Make a list of images, objects, words and phrases that are haunting in some way.
   b Now think of some adjectives or descriptions that would make your list of words and phrases even more effective. Refer to all your senses.
   c Extend your images and ideas so you have a series of related images.
   d Decide whether you will write in free verse or not and then test out a few lines.

   For example:

A window flings open, an all-seeing eye
Discordant chords crash in my mind
Scraping memories from view

   e Now write your whole poem.

Taking it further

Read 'The Raven' and 'The Pit and the Pendulum' by Edgar Allan Poe.

Write a story involving a haunting.

How did I do?

✔

I know that a haunting atmosphere can be created by selecting words or images that convey fear. ☐

I know that extending metaphors can intensify this atmosphere. ☐

I know that inexplicable things are often the most haunting. ☐

I know that poems can be written in structured stanzas or free verse. ☐

18: 'The Dream Woman'

Get started

Taking on the voice of a character from a text requires you to put yourself in his or her position and to adopt his or her language.

Practice

1 Which of these sentences sound as if they come from a story set in the past?

    a He didn't want to come to the cinema.
    b The servant-girl takes after her misuses.
    c It was nigh on twenty minutes past two.
    d She flicked through the magazine.

2 Which words helped you to make your decisions?

Challenge

Read this extract adapted from Wilkie Collins' short story 'The Dream Woman'. Isaac, a stable hand, is staying at an inn overnight when a strange vision appears to him.

The first sensation of which he was conscious after sinking into slumber was a strange shivering that ran through him suddenly from head to foot, and a dreadful sinking pain at the heart, such as he had never felt before. In one moment he passed from a state of sleep to a state of wakefulness – his eyes wide open – his mental perceptions cleared on a sudden, as if by a miracle.

The candle had burnt down nearly to the last morsel of tallow, but the light in the little room was, for the moment, fair and full.

Between the foot of his bed and the closed door there stood a woman with a knife in her hand, looking at him.

He was stricken speechless with terror, but he did not lose the preternatural clearness of his faculties, and he never took his eyes off the woman. She said not a word as they stared each other in the face, but she began to move slowly toward the left-hand side of the bed.

His eyes followed her. She was a fair, fine woman, with yellowish flaxen hair and light gray eyes, with a droop in the left eyelid. Speechless, with no expression in her face, with no noise following her footfall, she came closer and closer – stopped – and slowly raised the knife. He laid his right arm over his throat to save it; but, as he saw the knife coming down, threw his hand across the bed to the right side, and jerked his body over that way just as the knife descended on the mattress within an inch of his shoulder.

His eyes fixed on her arm and hand as she slowly drew her knife out of the bed: a white, well-shaped arm, with a pretty down lying lightly over the fair skin – a delicate lady's hand, with the crowning beauty of a pink flush under and round the finger nails.

As she approached she raised the knife again and he drew himself away to the left side. She struck, as before, right into the mattress, with a deliberate, perpendicularly-downward action of the arm. His eyes wandered from her to the knife. For the second time, she drew the knife out, concealed it in the wide sleeve of her gown, then stopped by the bedside, watching him. For an instant he saw her standing in that position, then the wick of the spent candle fell over into the socket; the flame diminished to a little blue point, and the room grew dark.

3 What strange feeling woke Isaac?

4 Find some words and phrases that suggest Isaac's fear.

5 Describe what Isaac saw.

When Isaac wakes the landlord of the inn and claims that a woman has tried to kill him, they discover that his bedroom window and door are still locked shut and the mattress into which a knife is supposed to have plunged is untouched. The landlord concludes that the image was a dream and chides Isaac for disturbing the house with his madness. Isaac is disturbed by this and is left to think about the events of the night.

6 You are going to write Isaac's diary entry the next day.

   a First, make a list of the points that you will include – what events will you refer to?
   b Now, think about how Isaac feels and what his thoughts may be. Write down your thoughts.

Read the following two extracts from attempts at diary entries.

He was upset and could not believe what had happened to him. Who had that woman been and had he imagined her? How could that be true when she had seemed so real to him?

What vision was this that visited me last night? My discoveries after she had gone told me that she had been nothing more than a figment of my imagination. Yet, I cannot deny what my eyes observed.

7 Which sounds more like a diary entry and why?

8 Which sounds like it is from the same time as 'The Dream Woman' and why?

9 Write Isaac's diary entry. Think carefully about your language as you write.

Taking it further

Read the whole of Wilkie Collins' story (copies can be found on the internet).

Write another diary entry for Isaac at the end of the story.

How did I do?

I know that when writing the diary entry of a character I should imagine that I am this person. ☐

I know that I should refer to events, thoughts and feelings, and write in the first person. ☐

I know that I should use the language that the character would use. ☐

19: Who dunnit?

In this unit you will explore:
- how to write the opening to a Sherlock Holmes detective story.

Get started

Detective stories engage readers' interests through a combination of mystery and suspense.

Practice

1. Make a list of features that you think are essential in a detective story. For example, a crime is necessary.

2. Make a list of detectives you have come across from television or books; for example, Inspector Poirot.

3. What do these detectives have in common?

Challenge

Before you start to read some Sherlock Holmes stories, go to the Sherlock Holmes Museum's site (www.sherlock-holmes.co.uk). Take the museum tour and make notes for future reference.

Read the following extract from 'The Adventure of the Blue Carbuncle', a Sherlock Holmes story by Sir Arthur Conan Doyle.

I had called upon my friend Sherlock Holmes upon the second morning after Christmas, with the intention of wishing him the compliments of the season. He was lounging upon the sofa in a purple dressing-gown, a pipe-rack within his reach upon the right, and a pile of crumpled morning papers, evidently newly studied, near at hand. Beside the couch was a wooden chair, and on the angle of the back hung a very seedy and disreputable hard-felt hat, much the worse for wear and cracked in several places. A lens and a forceps lying upon the seat of the chair suggested that the hat had been suspended in this manner for the purpose of examination.

'You are engaged,' said I; 'perhaps I interrupt you.'

'Not at all. I am glad to have a friend with whom I can discuss my results. The matter is a perfectly trivial one' – he jerked his thumb in the direction of the old hat – 'but there are points in connection with it which are not entirely devoid of interest and even of instruction.'

I seated myself in his armchair and warmed my hands before his crackling fire, for a sharp frost had set in, and the windows were thick with the ice crystals. 'I suppose,' I remarked, 'that, homely as it looks, this thing has some deadly story linked on to it – that it is the clue which will guide you in the solution of some mystery and the punishment of some crime.'

4. Who do you think is narrating the story?

5. What is the setting of the story? Find words and phrases linked to the setting.

6 What clue is introduced to the story? Find the line where it is first introduced.

Later in the story, Holmes provides his deductions about the owner of this object, as adapted below.

> He picked it up and gazed at it in the peculiar introspective fashion which was characteristic of him. 'That the man was highly intellectual is of course obvious upon the face of it, and also that he was fairly well-to-do within the last three years, although he has now fallen upon evil days. He had foresight, but has less now than formerly, pointing to a moral retrogression, which, when taken with the decline of his fortunes, seems to indicate some evil influence, probably drink, at work upon him. This may account also for the obvious fact that his wife has ceased to love him. He has, however, retained some degree of self-respect. He is a man who leads a sedentary life, goes out little, is out of training entirely, is middle-aged, has grizzled hair which he has had cut within the last few days, and which he anoints with lime-cream. These are the more patent facts which are to be deduced from his hat. Also, by the way, that it is extremely improbable that he has gas laid on in his house.'

7 Summarise the conclusions Holmes makes about the owner of the object.

8 Read the rest of the story to find out why Holmes makes these deductions. (The story can be found on the internet.)

9 Using a similar formula to 'The Adventure of the Blue Carbuncle', write the opening of a Sherlock Holmes story. Remember to focus on setting, introduction of a clue and dialogue between Watson and Holmes. Also remember whose voice to use as a narrator.

Taking it further

Develop your opening into a full-length story. Plan what will happen in the rest of the story and write it.

How did I do?

I know that Sherlock Holmes stories are narrated by Watson. ☐

I know that they involve crimes that need to be solved, and open with a clue and Holmes's deductions. ☐

I know that when writing a Sherlock Holmes opening I need to focus on creating a setting, introducing the first clue and developing the conversation between Holmes and Watson about the clue and the case. ☐

20: Quality not quantity

In this unit you will explore:
- how to write a 250-word short story
- how to write a mini saga (a 50-word story).

Get started

Writing to a set word limit requires you to choose the best words and write with precision.

Practice

1 Look at the pairs of words listed below. What is the difference between the words in each of the pairs?

get – retrieve	see – scrutinise	walk – amble	sad – depressed
red – crimson	hard – coarse	sporty – agile	smelly – fragrant

Challenge

Read the following 250-word story.

May had never seen the sun.

'It disappeared after the first explosion,' her grandmother said. 'A huge mushroom cloud grew above us; its dust fell down from the sky one piece at a time.' She cast her eyes down. 'To this day, I can still see it – that blanket of dust. I was indoors, the heat so intense my face blistered as sure as if my skin had been fried.'

May looked up at her grandmother; the scarred skin and vacant eyes stared past her.

'That blast took the light away.'

She nodded and stroked her grandmother's hair. 'Took more than that,' May said.

'That it did. Why your Grandpa, he was a fine man. Head and shoulders above any other. That man was all heart, and your ma . . .'

A tear traced its way down her cheek.

'Out of doors when it happened – he and your ma getting into that rust bucket. I'd just waved 'em off and, you, you were just a baby in my arms.' She sighed. 'Forty years, May. It's been forty years – of darkness and cold, and now this.'

She smiled serenely.

'I can feel the warmth again, May, and God willing, now, your darkness will end.'

'Ah, Grandma, I wish you could see it,' May said, taking hold of her grandmother's hand, but just as she did it slipped from hers, and those vacant eyes slid shut.

May looked at the light in the sky, and back at her grandmother. 'Now our darkness has ended,' she said.

2 What happens in the story?

3 Who are the characters?

4 Identify any words from the story that you think are particularly precise or well chosen and explain why you think this.

5 What do you understand by 'Now our darkness has ended'?

6 Being able to write concisely is a key skill when your word limit is small. Look at the phrases listed below and think of substitute single words.

   a make something sound bigger or better than it is e________

   b unnecessarily long winded v________

   c can be seen through t________

   d make something clearer so that it is understood c________

   e draw attention to something h________

   f fall over something t________

7 Think of your own plot for a short story. Limit yourself to one or two characters and a simple plot based on a haunted house. Write your story. If it runs over 250 words try to make phrases more concise, or cut them completely.

Reduce your 250-word story to 50 words.

Taking it further

Reduce the following 70 words to a 50-word mini saga.

> It was late in the evening. The stars shone down from the sky and the moon beamed down on us. We were driving through the night to the hotel. The car rattled its way along the deserted and dark road. The light beams flickered on and off and the road was eerily quiet. We were approaching a fork in the road when the car spluttered and came to a halt.

How did I do?

☐ I know that in order to write a 250-word short story I have to choose my words carefully.

☐ I know that a mini saga is a 50-word story.

☐ I know that when writing a mini saga, I should limit myself to one or two characters and straightforward action.

21: All about me

Get started

Autobiographical accounts are narrative descriptions about a person's real life written by the person him- or herself. Whilst these accounts are factually true, writers may embellish and exaggerate sections to entertain their readers.

Practice

1 Identify which are facts and which opinions in the following sentences.

   a It was Tuesday evening.
   b *X Factor* is an awful show.
   c The road wound to the left.
   d The car spluttered to a halt.
   e Chelsea is the best football team ever.
   f Tom Cruise is a top actor.

Challenge

Read the following extract taken from Amy Tan's book *The Opposite of Fate*.

After two weeks in Holland, we took a train to Germany and landed in Karlsruhe, where we lived as guests of a U.S. Army chaplain, an old friend of my father's. We attended an American school, where students thought it a fun prank to aim lit Bunsen burners at one another. This, I told my mother, was not the kind of education she had had in mind when she had envisioned us studying abroad. With that, she bought a Volkswagen Beetle and a handbook of English-speaking schools, and off we went, heading south, letting ourselves be guided purely by the twists and turns of European highways.

By such maps of fate, we wound up in Montreux, Switzerland, at the shores of Lake Geneva. In this resort town, my mother quickly found our new home, a fully furnished chalet, complete with cuckoo clock and feather-tick beds, renting for the equivalent of one hundred U.S. dollars a month. The largest room served as living room, dining room, and my brother's bedroom, and its entire length was lined with mullioned windows showcasing a spectacular view of the lake and the Alps. Every day, I would stare at this amazing scenery and wonder how I came to be so lucky. I would then remember that my father and older brother were dead, and that was the reason I was here.

Half a mile from our chalet, down a cobblestone path, lay an international school. It was within eyesight of Château de Chillon, where the dashing Lord Byron was said to have chained himself to write his poetry in religious agony. By happy chance, there were two openings for day students. My mother weighed the benefits of a four-to-one pupil–teacher ratio, the mandatory ski outings as physical education, the private piano lessons and one-to-one drawing classes, the Spanish teacher from Spain, the French teacher from France, and English teachers from England, and decided it was all worth the extravagant cost of six hundred dollars per year.

2 Identify words and sentences from the extract that sound factual (true) and any words or phrases that seem to have been exaggerated or are written to entertain.

3 Write some facts about your own life.

4 Look at the following sentences.

- By such maps of fate, we wound up in Montreux, Switzerland, at the shores of Lake Geneva.
- It ended up that we arrived in Switzerland.

What is the difference between these two sentences?

5 Find some details from the passage that add interest but are not entirely necessary to the factual account.

6 Add interest to your facts from question 3.

7 Amy Tan refers to events, settings, conversations and thoughts. Isolate where each of these appears in the passage.

8 Amy Tan uses carefully chosen vocabulary. Select four or five verbs and adjectives that you think are effective and explain why you think this.

9 You are going to write your own autobiographical account, using some of Amy Tan's techniques. Decide on a particular episode from your life on which you will focus.

a Create a spidergram of ideas related to this episode.

Setting: Where? When?

Thoughts?

Events: Who was involved? Why?

incident

Conversations?

Entertaining parts?

Descriptive details?

b Write your opening sentence. Make it as engaging as possible. If it doesn't sound great, don't worry. Go back to it later.
c Write about one side of A4 in total. Remember to use effective verbs and adjectives, possibly humour and some imagery, such as metaphors.

How did I do?

✔

I know that creative non-fiction accounts are true stories that employ narrative or poetic devices to entertain readers. ☐

I know that creative non-fiction is about a true event, but includes dialogue, thoughts, descriptive detail and carefully selected vocabulary. ☐

22: How? What? Why?

Get started

An instruction manual guides people in how to do something. It is organised and easy to follow.

An explanatory article uses both words and images to give details about a particular topic.

Practice

1. Which of the following do you think are needed in a manual and which are more likely be found in an explanatory article?

   - step-by-step instructions
   - clear language
   - details
   - history
   - technical jargon
   - facts and figures
   - reasons

Challenge

Instruction manual

Read this extract taken from a DIY instruction manual.

How to fix a leaking tap

There are two kinds of tap mechanism: Washer and Ceramic disc.

Washer taps are available in a wide variety of styles but they all work in the same way. Turning the handle closes a washer against the water inlet inside the tap, shutting off the supply. With reverse pressure taps ('Supataps') you can fix a leaking washer without having to turn the water off. However, it is always preferable to turn off the water supply before you start.

Ceramic disc taps have revolving discs instead of washers. They usually go from off to fully on in a quarter turn, making them convenient for elderly or disabled people. Wear is less of a problem than with washer taps, but if there is a problem you have to replace a disc cartridge, which is more expensive than fitting a washer.

2. Look at the first line of the extract. What has the writer done here?

3. In terms of subject, how does the writer divide his paragraphs?

4. Look at the first lines of the two main paragraphs. What does the writer do in each of these?

5. Look at the extract as a whole. Identify the sentences where the main instructions appear.

6 You are going to write a set of instructions for how to take a picture with a digital camera or mobile phone camera and download it onto a computer to print. Look back at the extract from a manual shown opposite. Use this structure and layout to help you.

    a Make a note of each step that you make when taking and downloading images.
    b Make sure that the steps are in the correct order so that someone else can follow them easily. Make sure that your language is clear.
    c Test that your instructions work and can be followed.
    d Provide some images to help the readers.

Explanatory article

When dinosaurs first appeared about 230 million years ago the world was very different. There were very few of the animal groups we recognise today – no mammals, no birds and no lizards.

What? No grass?
The difference was also apparent in the plant kingdom. Plant life would have seemed very drab. There were no flowering plants, so nothing like most of the common trees and shrubs today. There was no grass. Instead, low ground cover would have been ferns and mosses.

A giant desert
The continents of the Triassic Earth were configured differently to today. All the land masses on the planet were joined together into one huge continent called Pangaea. This stretched from pole to pole and its central region was a vast inhospitable desert.

New life
The Late Triassic was an innovative time in the animal kingdom. By the end of the period not only the dinosaurs had appeared but also pterosaurs (flying reptiles), various kinds of marine reptiles, the first crocodiles and turtles, and the earliest true mammals. Towards the end of the Triassic, 220 million years ago, there was another extinction, which wiped out many of the non-dinosaurs.

7 Look at the way the information is divided. Make a note of subheadings.

8 Explanatory writing relies a lot on nouns. From the text, make a list of common, proper and abstract nouns (at least two of each).

9 There are some specialist terms in this article. List a few of these words.

10 List any facts or figures in the article.

11 Whom do you think this article is aimed at and why?

Taking it further

Select a topic that you know well or have studied in school and decide on an audience that you will write for. Write an explanatory article for a website about your topic. Use a combination of words and images. Also, divide your article using subheadings. You might even provide links to explain jargon or for further reading.

How did I do?

          ✔

I know that an instruction manual is a clear set of instructions about how to do something. ☐

I know that an explanatory article is made up of text and images. ☐

I know that an explanatory article tells people about a topic and usually answers the questions what, how and why. ☐

23: Writing a PowerPoint presentation

In this unit you will explore:

- how to write a PowerPoint presentation for a charity.

Get started

Charities exist to help people in need. They might produce slideshows to promote their charity and persuade others to help them. Charities also use persuasive writing in order to get an emotional reaction from their readers.

Practice

1. Identify any emotive words in the following sentences.

    a. The despair that the children experience is seen in their eyes.
    b. The road was blocked.
    c. The cruel nature of the blast left many stranded, helpless and homeless.
    d. People spent hours clearing the road of debris.
    e. The bundles of litter crowded the otherwise barren wasteland.

Challenge

As well as using emotive language, charities may aim to persuade by using facts and figures, lists, rhetorical questions and pronouns addressing or including the audience ('you', 'we', 'us').

2. Read the following extract adapted from the Save the Children 'Rewrite the Future' campaign. What persuasive devices can you see?

43 million children are out of school because of conflict: Rewrite the future

'I am very proud to know how to count and read. I now say to all my young brothers not to get involved with the military. It's not good for the children.' Felix, 16, Côte d'Ivoire

Education saves lives. It gives children the skills they need to escape poverty, live healthily and have hope for the future. The right to go to school belongs to every child.

However, 115 million children are still out of primary school – that's 18 per cent of the world's primary-school-aged population. Save the Children research has shown that at least 43 million of these children – one in three – live in countries affected by conflict.

Ensuring children in conflict-affected countries get an education is one of the biggest challenges facing the international community. It's not easy, even for the major donors, to ensure that aid reaches children in countries where governments fail to make schooling a priority and where aid channels get blocked. But, for children in conflict situations, education is as important as healthcare and shelter. It should be a part of every emergency response and a priority in helping to repair and rebuild the lives of children in post-conflict situations.

We are calling on world leaders, international organisations, national governments and individuals to join us and help us rewrite the future for all the 43 million children being denied an education in countries affected by conflict.

3 Look back at the plan for a PowerPoint presentation that you did earlier, in Unit 15. You should have decided on a charity and have a clear plan of what you will include on each slide.

   a Write the slide about what your charity does. Remember to write in a clear and informative way.

   b You should have found some facts and figures about your charity. Arrange these so that they are easy to read and powerfully presented.

   c Now, write the slide that features a true story. You need to be persuasive here, so use some emotive language and rhetorical questions.

   d Finally, in the section about what people can do to help, you need to appeal to your readers, so using direct and inclusive pronouns like 'you', 'we' and 'us' will help. You could also use bullet points.

   e In planning the slideshow in Unit 15, you may have also planned a leaflet. Now, write the content of this leaflet to accompany your PowerPoint presentation.

Taking it further

Visit www.salvationarmy.org.uk and search for their 'PowerPoint presentations'. Look at the Belief in Action PowerPoint (or one of the other presentations) to gain an idea of how this charity presents itself in an informative way.

How did I do?

✔

I know that a charity might produce a slideshow on PowerPoint to inform people about the charity and persuade them to support it. ☐

I know that to write a PowerPoint presentation for a charity I should make sure that the information included is correct and that I am able to convey my ideas clearly and persuasively. ☐

24: A balancing act

Get started

A balanced analysis of a topic considers both sides and is written in an impartial and unbiased way.

Practice

1 Look at the following biased sentences. Identify which words make them sound biased.

   a Having to pay for a television licence is ludicrous.
   b The M25 is a nightmare road.
   c Public transport in the UK is a joke.
   d Capital punishment is inhumane.

2 Rewrite the sentences so that they sound unbiased.

Challenge

People have different opinions about whether or not computers are a good thing.

3 What reasons might people have for thinking computers are good?

4 What reasons might people have for thinking they aren't good?

Read the two extracts printed below. They are sections taken from two students' essays on the pros and cons of computers.

a Computers are good because they allow us to do things we wouldn't be able to do without them. They can calculate very difficult sums and carry out complicated tasks which we cannot. They are bad though because people lose jobs and computers aren't reliable as they crash.

b Some people believe that computers are a blessing: they allow us to carry out difficult and long calculations which we would otherwise have been unable to do. Calculating the answer to two million three hundred and seventy six multiplied by thirty seven thousand is no longer a problem now that we have computers to hand. However, computers are machines and as such they are prone to faults and problems. Sometimes they become infected with viruses. There are thousands of them out there. That's why McAfee software was invented, and sometimes computers crash. Another point raised against computers is the fact that they are starting to replace people. You don't have to stand in a queue to buy a train ticket from a person any more. You can buy one from a machine now. On the plus side companies are saving money but on the minus side people are losing their jobs.

5 The points that the two students make are similar. What are these points?

6   Extract **b** is better in terms of style. What words does the second student use to link her sentences together so that she moves from one point to another easily?

7   What else does the second student do that makes her writing better?

8   Match the words below with the function they carry out in an essay.

Words	Functions
Some people believe However Others think that On the other hand Similarly Likewise Whilst Whereas	Raising opponents' views Suggesting a contrast Suggesting a comparison, similarity

9   Make a list of points for and against school uniform.

10   Now, write an essay about school uniforms analysing the two sides. Remember to structure your essay by writing an introduction, main body and conclusion (see Unit 14).

You might start:

School uniform is a much debated topic. Some people believe that it provides a school with an easily recognisable identity, that it gets students in the right frame of mind for work and that it helps to prevent bullying. Others feel it is an outdated system that stunts individuality and prevents students from feeling relaxed and performing at their best.

Taking it further

Write an essay analysing the ways that modern life in Britain is both better and worse than it was 200 years ago. Remember to look at both sides of the topic, including both positive and negative things about life today. Also, provide specific examples to give your essay more weight.

How did I do?

✔

I know that analysing a topic in a balanced way means writing about both sides of a debate. ☐

I know that impartial language and examples should be used. ☐

25: Book reviewing

Get started

Critics review books for newspapers and magazines. A review is an article about a book, which includes subjective opinions and an indication of highlights and drawbacks.

Practice

1. Look at the list of words below and decide which suggest positive opinions and which suggest negative ones.

outstanding   clever   obscure   lengthy   slow   verbose
believable   predictable   dramatic   exciting   incomprehensible

2. Write a list of words that you could use to describe a scene or a character. Try to include both positive and negative words.

Challenge

Read the following review of Elizabeth Laird's book *Red Sky in the Morning*. This is a novel about Anna Peacock, a twelve-year-old girl, in whose voice the book is narrated.

The plot starts with Anna looking forward to the birth of her baby brother. However, when he arrives and Anna and her family are told that he is disabled, Anna's world is thrown into confusion. She grows to love her brother dearly but is ashamed of admitting the truth about Ben to her school friends. When the truth finally comes out things start to unfold even more. This novel is about Anna's trials and tribulations as she journeys through life to learn the values family holds, to face peer rivalry and to encounter her first romance. We see Anna mature as life throws one event after another in her path.

As with all of Elizabeth Laird's books, *Red Sky in the Morning* is beautifully written in clear prose with believable dialogue and action. Events pull at your heartstrings and there are times when even the most hardened teenager will have to reach for a tissue. As for Anna herself, she is a wholly accurate character. We grow to know her and feel for her misfortunes and successes. Her quirky sense of humour and open nature are entertaining and apt. Once again, Laird has created an excellent book. The issues she raises in the novel are timeless and, as with her other novels, this one is set to become a modern classic.

3. Look at the way this review is organised. Make a list of the different features included in the review and what is included in each paragraph.

4. Identify some words and phrases from the review that make the book sound as if it's worth reading.

5 How does the reviewer describe the target reader?

6 Is there anything else that you think should have been included in this review?

Reviewers, like any writers, have to consider their audience and their purpose. This tells them what sort of language to use – in other words what *register* to use.

7 You are going to write a book review. Try to read some that others have written.

   a Choose a book to review and then brainstorm some ideas. Your spidergram might look like this:

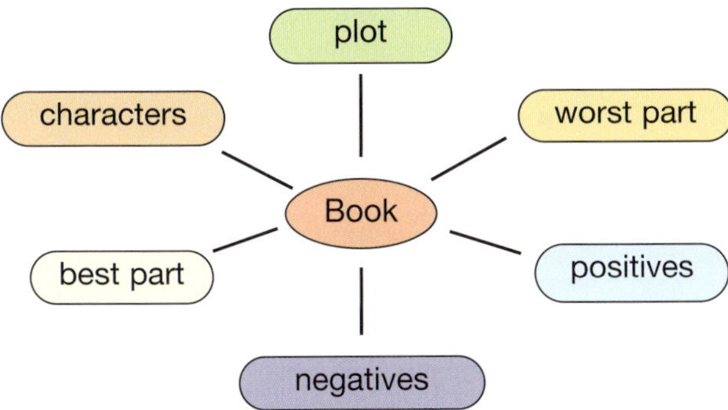

   b Write your review. Think about the kind of language you will use, and whether you will use the first or third person or a combination of both.

Taking it further

Send your book review to www.scholastic.co.uk/zone/reading_reviews-advice.htm.

How did I do?

                                  ✔

I know that book reviews give readers an indication of what a book is like. ☐

I know that a book review is one person's idea of what a book is like. ☐

I know that a book review should include a brief outline, highlights and drawbacks. ☐

I know that the first person, third person or a combination of both may be used. ☐

Answers

Unit 1

1 considerable, One may, companions, excessive, within the means, an extremely amusing diversion

2 Many people really enjoy going to the circus. You can go on your own or with friends. It's usually quite cheap and most families can afford it. It can be a great night out.

3a
- perhaps for a tourist guide or to claim protection for a particular church as being unique
- What period is covered by 'medieval'? What were the main styles? What technical advances were there? Who were the famous architects? What were the differences in style?
- internet, library
- Architecture and History

b
- for an art book or a biography
- When did he live? Where did he live? What is so good about his art? What kind of man was he?
- internet, library
- Art history

c
- for a local guide, or a talk to the local history society
- What industries or types of farming have there been? Was anyone famous born here? Did anyone famous come here? What buildings were here? What were the local customs?
- local library, possibly internet, local church or other old monument, old people, old maps
- local history

d
- to prepare for a holiday, or to write a book about ancient death rituals
- How was mummitication done? Why was it done? When was it done? What beliefs are associated with it?
- library, internet
- Egyptology

e
- to become a zoo keeper, to research animal intelligence
- Where do they live? What do they eat? What different types are there? Are they an endangered species? How intelligent are they?
- library, zoo, aquarium, internet
- Zoology

4

Passage 1	Passage 2
1. Son of a glovemaker	1. Son of a farm worker
2. Grammar School, where he learned Latin, logic and history	2. Classical university education, learning Greek and geography
3. We do not know exactly when and why he moved to London, but by 1592 he was known as a playwright.	3. Perhaps moved to London to escape a poaching charge. By 1590 was writing plays. (Not quite a contradiction, but nearly)
4. Supported by Earl of Salisbury	4. Supported by Earl of Southampton
5. Wife Anne was much younger	5. Anne was older
6. They had three children: two daughters and a son, Hamnet	6. Four children, including son Hamlet (plague and Black Death same)
7. Career interrupted by an outbreak of smallpox	7. Career interrupted by plague
8. Plays performed for Elizabeth I	8. Plays performed for James I (also true!)
9. Died 1513	9. Died 1514
10. Wrote 154 plays and 38 sonnets	10. Wrote 38 plays and 154 sonnets

Unit 2

1

Abbreviations: fridge (refrigerator); Col. (Colonel)
Contractions: Dr (Doctor)
Acronyms: BBC (British Broadcasting Corporation);
WYSIWYG (What You See Is What You Get – referring to a
computer program); nimby (not in my backyard – for someone
who is not against something in principle but does not want it
in their locality, e.g. a wind farm or a prison); scuba (self-
contained underwater breathing apparatus)

2   This is down to personal views, but a spidergram is
probably the easiest to add to and organise an essay
from. Underlining is good for key words in a news article.
Cards keep main headings separate. Linear notes are
easy to make, especially if you don't know where a talk is
going.

3   **a** possibly a spidergram, though linear notes can work
   b possibly linear notes
   c a spidergram or cards
   d linear notes; perhaps underlining if it's your book!

4   There are several causes of climate change, including
greenhouse gases such as carbon monoxide and carbon
dioxide. These are emitted by factory chimneys, car
exhausts and cows, and result in an overall rise in global
temperature. However, this is not uniform across the
world. Africa will be the hardest hit. There is further
variation in that some parts of the world will receive more
rainfall, while some will suffer increasingly from drought.
The rise in temperature will cause the polar ice caps to
melt, leading to a rise in sea levels and consequent
flooding of low-lying areas. Wildlife will be affected, most
obviously animals such as polar bears. Part of the
solution is to make drastic cuts in the consumption of
unnecessary products such as plastic wrappers. This
would be good for everyone.

Unit 3

1   **a** Skateboarding, now popular in many parts of the
   world, started in California in the 1950s, with surfers
   trying to surf the streets.
   b Lacrosse, a game in which players attempt to scoop up
   a ball and throw it into the opponents' goal, was
   invented by Native Americans, who regarded it as good
   military training.

2   These sources could be combined in many ways. Check
that your version contains all the important points, in a
sensible order, and does not repeat anything.

Unit 4

1   This is not a definitive list, but the matches below make
sense.

Symbolic object	Theme
sword	hate (though Buddhists see it as a symbol of truth)
wall	divided communities
unicorn	magic
pen	truth (or knowledge)
fist	resistance to oppression
mountains	knowledge (or the mystery of universe)
whale	the mystery of the universe

2   Mr Pedanski's attitude towards Zero is very negative, and
is especially unworthy of someone who is supposed to be
helping the boys to become useful members of society. His
low expectations of Zero do not help Zero to achieve
anything.

3   Stanley believes in Zero's ability to learn.

4   education, literacy, the power of authority

5   He is saying that people may be more intelligent and able
to learn than they appear to be, and that they should be
encouraged to learn.

6   Gradgrind gives her no chance to show what she knows.
He is dismissive towards her.

7   the purpose of education

8   education

9   Sachar explores personal potential; Dickens does this to
some extent but is more interested in what education is
for – the mechanical categorisation of mostly useless
facts, or something else.

Unit 5

2   They feel they should support each other and share what
they have.

3   Ephraim is ashamed because he feels he should be self-
sufficient and not have to accept charity.

4   The miners shared hardship and danger underground and
the strike is a shared fight for more pay, so they unite in
the face of Ephraim's loss.

5   **a** Falstaff thinks honour is worthless, especially if you're
   dead. The opposite would be if someone was prepared
   to risk their life for the sake of honour.
   b Siward thinks that the most important thing for a man
   is to die bravely. The opposite would be to think one
   should attempt to stay alive at all costs.
   c Claudio thinks that women should be virgins, and
   probably not even kiss a man before they marry. He
   feels justified in hurting his bride Hero and ruining her
   reputation on 'evidence' that she has broken this code.
   The opposite would perhaps be to expect no more of
   women than of men in this respect, and perhaps to
   think that virginity in itself was not important.

Unit 6

1 a The education was very poor.
  b A shop doorway is not much of a home.
  c It was not really a surprise.
2 a fact
  b opinion
  c fact
  d fact
  e opinion
  f fact (they *did* think it)
3 a Gorillas like to eat large quantities of fruit.
  b Elephants can spray themselves using their trunks.
  c Mickey Mouse is a lovable cartoon character.
  d It is against the law to impersonate a police officer.
  e Abraham Lincoln was President of the United States.
  f Professional footballers have excellent ball control.
4 The first article claims that the Prime Minister is almost lying; it also interprets figures as showing that street crime is out of control. It regards 2,305 unsolved muggings as a high figure and suggests (without offering any evidence) that it would be even higher if people were not too afraid to go out, and didn't have so little faith in the police that they do not bother to report crime. It does not mention the total number of muggings. This article does not support the Prime Minister. The phrases 'explain away' and 'massively' suggest bias.

The second article claims that the Prime Minister 'has welcomed' these figures and that they actually reflect an increase in the public reporting of crime, which in turn is the result of increased confidence in the police. It thinks that 2,305 is a low figure, compared with the total of 4,000. This article supports the Prime Minister. The phrases 'welcomed' and 'increased public confidence' suggest bias.

Unit 7

1 a Friendly and informal; uses slang and careless exaggeration.
  b Formal; uses words that come from Latin, such as 'inform' rather than 'tell', and 'require' rather than 'need'. It is also slightly long-winded.
  c Ironic and understated; it is clear that the author does not respect the President although he says that he does.
  d Romantic; uses words such as 'enfolded', 'trembling', 'manly' and 'sighed'.
2 The tone is understated and reasonable: 'full agreement', 'necessary explanations'.
3 'Many of us actually dislike milk and apples.'
4 'Milk and apples (this has been proved by Science, comrades) contain substances absolutely necessary to the well-being of a pig.' Of course he does not say what those 'substances' are!

5 the fear that Jones the farmer will return
6 Orwell describes him childishly 'skipping from side to side and whisking his tail'.
7 Most critics think it works well.
8 The pigs and humans have become identical – symbolising the way in which, in Orwell's eyes, the leaders who emerged from the Russian Revolution of 1917, like Stalin, became just as corrupt, self-seeking and greedy as the leaders of the previous regime, and the leaders of other capitalist (non-Communist) countries.

Unit 8

1 a I tried to cast my tackle into the centre of the stream. I might find a fish there.
  b She was beautiful. More important, she was brave. Both of these are desirable features in a trapeze artist.
  c I entered the room with an attempt at dignity. However, I trod on a toy train. The train had been abandoned by Ben. I skidded across the floor. I then landed in a heap. I looked like a clown.
2 It says the island is 'a mystery'.
3 They are relaxed. They are chatting casually. Whitney makes a joke.
4 He does this so that there will be a contrast when things start to go wrong. It also suggests that things can go wrong even when we are feeling secure.
5 They are in the tropics, passing an island. They are both hunters. Rainsford has good eyesight and is an excellent shot with a rifle.
6 The mood becomes more urgent. There is fast-moving action.
7 The reference to blood ('blood-warm waters') suggests that something life-threatening may occur.
8 Only one animal can reason. Read the story!
9 This is uncertain at this point, but it seems likely that he will encounter danger.

Unit 9

1 The first uses short, plain sentences; the second uses longer sentences, metaphors and more vivid verbs ('crept', 'hanging', 'flickering').
2 It makes us wonder what sort of strange creature is pursuing her.
3 The verbs tend to suggest brisk activity; e.g. 'leap', 'raked', 'scrambled'. The word 'raked' is quite unusual.
4 Susan's
5 'A spear *sighed* over her shoulder.' This makes us hear the sound of the spear in the air very close to Susan. The word 'sighed' is a surprising choice as it makes the spear sound almost harmless.
6 The description of the creature is interesting, and emphasises that the scene is seen from Susan's

viewpoint. The phrase 'pecking strides' suggests a brittle way of walking; saying 'the feet were taloned' is somehow more sinister than 'He had taloned feet'.

7 The verbs in Extract **b** are also active, though more dramatic than mysterious – e.g. 'leapt' and 'swooped'. The narrative viewpoint is partly objective – just the author telling the story (as with the details about the snowmobiles, which Alex couldn't really know in these circumstances). Garner makes the pursuit seem urgent by revealing the strangeness of the creature and the closeness of the spear. Horowitz emphasises the technology and the straightforward physical danger, without any sense of mystery. Horowitz uses one quite vivid metaphor: 'black flies swimming into his field of vision' to describe the men on snowmobiles.

Unit 10

1 **a** She has plenty of money.
   b I saw some police officers coming so I ran away.
   c I polished the knocker and it became pleasingly shiny.
   d Wait for a short time and he will probably come.

2 'cold and grey, exceedingly cold and grey'; 'no sun nor hint of sun'; 'the absence of sun . . . the lack of sun'. Both examples are for emphasis. They may also suggest the monotonous nature of the landscape.

3 'It was nine o'clock. There was no sun nor hint of sun, though there was not a cloud in the sky.'

4 touch and sight ('cold and grey'; 'a subtle gloom')

5 They are 'fat'.

6 The sun is 'cheerful'.

7 'There was no sun nor hint of sun, though there was not a cloud in the sky. It was a clear day, and yet there seemed an intangible pall over the face of things, a subtle gloom that made the day dark, and that was due to the absence of sun.' London's is more literary because of phrases like 'an intangible pall' and 'a subtle gloom'. And 'face of things' is an example of personification – albeit not a very obvious one.

8 London wants us to think that the man may come to grief through being too casual and self-confident about the cold.

9 The continuation is literary because of an imaginative choice of words; for example, 'flung a look', rather than just 'looked', and because of the vivid picture of the white landscape – 'pure white, rolling in gentle undulations' with the trail represented just as vividly in a metaphor as a 'dark hair-line'. There is also a build-up of sentences suggesting the great distance that the trail covers.

Unit 11

1 zoology, etymology, entomology, psychology, biology, toxicology, radiology

2 arachnophobia (spiders), agoraphobia (open spaces), demophobia (crowds). See also: http:// phobialist.com.

3 • poor people: little sympathy for the poor (**b** and **c**)
   • children: should be quiet and tidy, may be hit (**b** and **c**)
   • schoolgirls: should be humble, quiet and tidy (**c**)
   • religion: only Christians are civilised (**a** and **c**); it is the duty of Christians to educate others in 'Christian' virtues, such as humility, even if it makes them suffer (**c**)
   • exploration: it is exciting and there is much to discover (**a**)
   • foreigners: many are 'wild, bloodthirsty savages' (**a**)

4 **a** It shows that Jews were hated and persecuted.
   b Shakespeare's attitude seems more sympathetic in that this is a powerful speech which creates sympathy for the character, but he did not go out of his way to portray Shylock as a good man.

Unit 12

1 The use of the present tense makes the moment seem more important and almost dreamlike. The use of the future tense at the end creates a feeling of anticipation – wanting the question answered.

2 **a** adventure (could also be crime)
   b science fiction
   c horror
   d crime

3 **a** the dangerous action, but also the active words such as 'hurled' and dramatic phrases like 'twisted in a mask of fury'
   b the emphasis on aliens, planets and futuristic technology
   c the moon, the graveyard setting, the false sense of security – we assume that there is something horrible and unnatural about the child
   d the tough, worldly character of the officer in charge, the crime scene details, the expectation of some peculiar clue at the end

4 This is comedy sci-fi (like *The Hitchhiker's Guide to the Galaxy*).

Unit 13

1 Stresses are as follows.
   a By the shining Big-Sea-Water (four pairs of stressed and unstressed)
   b O what can ail thee, knight-at-arms (four pairs of unstressed and stressed)
   c Like the leaves of the forest when Summer is green (four triplets of two unstressed and one stressed)

2 It sounds like Native American drums.

3 Byron's poem does. It fits the Assyrians attacking on horseback.

4   Keats's poem. The fourth line makes it seem as if something is wrong or is fading away – like the sick knight.
5   only the second and fourth lines of each verse
6   It rhymes in couplets: AA BB, etc. This helps to create the effect of a strong, unstoppable force driving down on Sennacherib.
7   A haiku has three lines, consisting of five, seven and five syllables.

Unit 14

1   sly, dirty, slimy, vermin, disease, beady eyes, whiskers
2   He feels sorry for him and knows what it is like to hitchhike.
3   He is kind and empathetic.
4, and 5

Quotation from the text	What this shows
'Going to London, guv'nor?'	man is probably a Cockney
'ratty-faced man with grey teeth'	sly, doesn't take care of teeth
'eyes were dark and quick'	sly but clever
'He didn't seem to like that question'	had something to hide
'he was wearing a greyish-coloured jacket with enormous pockets'	hints at his 'profession'

6   Introduction: **b**

Main body: **a**

Conclusion: **c**

Unit 15

1   Cancer Research Fund, RSPCA, NSPCC, Age Concern
2   'Thousands of people die'; 'take for granted'; 'Little Joshu'; 'over two miles away'
3   the use of colour, separate sections, short paragraphs to read, subheadings
4   names and photographs
5   Giving children back their future.
6   **a** 'We offer a wide range of support services for children, young people and their families, helping children who are young carers, for example, looking after a sick or disabled relative.'
    b 'Our website will tell you more about our work and how you can help children like these young carers.'
7   donating £2 per month, one-off cash gift online, sponsoring a child, fostering and adoption, Barnado's projects in your area, volunteer for Barnado's

Unit 16

1   Hansel and Gretel; Goldilocks; Red Riding Hood; Cinderella; Snow White; Rapunzel
3   First extract – original; second extract – parody
4   The parody has modern references like '*OK!* magazine', and 'football star'.
5   • Cinderella's stepfamily has been invited to the ball.
    • They will not let Cinderella attend.
    • Her fairy godmother arrives.
    • She uses her magic to create a carriage and dress for Cinderella and tells her to go to the ball but she must be back by midnight.
    • Cinderella goes to the ball and meets Prince Charming, but as the clock strikes midnight she rushes out leaving her shoe behind.
    • The prince is in love with Cinderella so he keeps her shoe as a clue to her identity.
    • He sends a messenger to all the houses with the shoe.
    • When the messenger arrives at Cinderella's house, her stepsisters rush around trying to fit their feet into her shoe.
    • Cinderella is able to fit her foot into the shoe and she and Prince Charming marry and live happily ever after.
6   exaggeration, understatement, ridiculous situations, word play, stating the obvious, detail
7   It is modernised and makes use of exaggeration.
8   The names of the characters are stereotypes; it draws on stereotypes of modern times – frivolous and shallow women; the word 'trap' is humorous; the contrast between 'tall, dark and handsome' and 'stupid' creates humour.

Unit 17

1   haunting – something that leaves a lasting memory, that is evocative or scary
2   a dusty mirror, a forgotten tune playing itself on a piano, a distant cry, the turning pages of a book, a window banging (some of the others in the right environment)
3   moonlight, the bars, the woman behind it is as plain as can be
5   'owl's call' – haunting sound; 'soon they'll be ruffled' – idea of chaos; 'slow gleam' – spooky atmosphere; 'human cry' – scary; 'wild hand', 'witchcraft, bedevilled' – cursed/ haunted people
6   alliteration and onomatopoeia: 'scrapes the stillness'; alliteration: 'lawns are levelled'; 'cry cuts across a dream'; 'curtains are barriers and behind them/The beds settle'
7   a rhyming pattern across the stanzas
8   call scrapes stillness; curtains are barriers; human cry cuts across a dream.

Unit 18

1   **b** and **c**
2   The servant-girl takes after her misuses.
    It was nigh on twenty minutes past two.
3   A strange shivering that ran from head to foot and a sinking pain in his heart.
4   'In one moment he passed from a state of sleep to a state of wakefulness'; 'stricken speechless with terror'; 'he drew himself away to the left side'
5   He saw a woman who angled a knife towards him, into the mattress, as if trying to kill him.
7   The second – it's written in the first person using 'me', 'my' and 'I'.
8   The second – the language is more in keeping with an older text.

Unit 19

1   crime, solution, detective, assistant, magnifying glass, tension, clues, witnesses, crime scene
2   Miss Marple, Inspector Clueso, Frost, Holmes
3   They often have assistants. They are intelligent and able to work out solutions from clues. They live alone, and are unmarried.
4   Dr Watson
5   indoors – 'the second morning after Christmas', 'lounging upon the sofa', 'a pile of crumpled morning papers', 'crackling fire'
6   hat: 'hung a very seedy and disreputable hard-felt hat'
7   He is intelligent. He used to be rich but isn't now. He used to be a forward thinking man. His life has gone downhill, perhaps because of drink. His wife no longer loves him. He is middle aged. He uses lime cream in his hair, has had his hair cut recently and he has no gas at home.

Unit 20

1   'retrieve' is to get back; 'scrutinise' is to look closely or examine; 'amble' is to walk slowly; 'depressed' suggests a stronger sadness than the word 'sad'; 'crimson' is a shade of red; 'coarse' is rough, 'hard' is solid; 'agile' is nimble and able to move easily; 'sporty' indicates a fondness for sport; 'fragrant' suggests a nice smell
2   The sun appears for the first time in 40 years.
    May sees it for the first time and her grandmother dies.
3   May and her grandmother
4   'mushroom cloud' – shape and texture; 'blistered' – sounds painful, indicates heat also; 'vacant' – empty of what? Leads us to think of many things.
5   Literally the darkness has ended but also metaphorically the sadness, or lack of hope, has ended.
6   **a** exaggerate
    b verbose
    c transparent
    d clarify
    e highlight
    f trip

Unit 21: All about me

1   Facts: **a**, **c**, **d**
    Opinions: **b**, **e**, **f**
2   Factual: 'After two weeks in Holland . . . father's'; 'We attended an American school'; The largest room served as living room . . . Alps'
    Exaggerated/to entertain: 'where students thought it a fun prank to aim lit Bunsen burners at one another'; 'guided purely by the twists and turns of European highways'; 'extravagant cost of six hundred dollars'
4   The first sentence uses more detail and a metaphor – 'maps of fate'; it also mentions Lake Geneva which we imagine is beautiful.
5   fun prank played by students; cuckoo clock and feather-tick beds; mullioned windows; mandatory ski outings
7   To help you: events – what happens; setting – place and time; conversations – with her mum; thoughts – narrator's views
8   Verbs: 'landed', 'wound up' – sound unplanned; 'lined' – gives a visual impression; 'chained' – humorous.
    adjectives: 'lit' Bunsen burners – suggests danger; 'fully furnished' chalet – a home from home

Unit 22

1   Manual: step-by-step instructions, clear language, technical jargon
    Article: clear language, details, history, facts and figures, reasons
2   He explains the two different taps he will discuss.
3   One is about washer taps, the other about ceramic disc taps.
4   He gives brief information about each kind of tap.
5   'Turning the handle . . . shutting off the supply'; 'With reverse . . . the water off.'
    'They usually go from . . . people'; 'if there is a problem you have to replace a disc cartridge'.
7   What? No grass?; A giant desert; New life
8   Common nouns: dinosaurs, world, mammals
    Proper nouns: Earth, Triassic, Pangaea
    Abstract nouns: time, period, extinction etc.
9   Pangaea, Triassic
10 For example: Dinosaurs first appeared about 230 million years ago.
11 Audience: children interested in history and biology. The material is broken down into small and easily digested chunks. It is quite easy to understand, with some words explained.

Unit 23

1   **a** despair, **b** blocked, **c** cruel, blast, stranded, helpless, homeless, **d** debris, **e** bundles, barren wasteland
2   '43 million' – fact; quotation from a person; 'saves', 'It's not easy' – emotive; 'should be' – guilt-inducing; 'we', 'us' – inclusive pronouns; lists

Unit 24

1   **a** ludicrous, **b** nightmare, **c** joke, **d** inhumane
2   **a** Some people disagree with having to pay for a television licence.
    b The M25 gets congested and some people dislike travelling on it.
    c Public transport in the UK is criticised by some people for being unreliable.
    d Some people think capital punishment is not a justifiable punishment.
3   They make tasks easier; efficiency; speed; multiple calculations are possible; word-processing; desk-top publishing and other software; fewer queues in some situations
4   They replace humans; people lose jobs; they can break down; they can develop viruses; difficult to fix if you don't know how; expensive to buy
5   easy to do long calculations; machines develop faults; people lose jobs
6   'However'; 'Another point'; 'On the plus side'
7   refers to 'you', making it personal to reader; refers to specific software; gives examples
8   Raising opponents' views: Some people believe; Others think that
    Suggesting a contrast: However; On the other hand; Whilst; Whereas
    Suggesting a comparison, similarity: Similarly; Likewise
9   For: gets students into work frame of mind; prepares students for later life; students look smart – representing school; gives students a sense of identity; makes it easier to identify a student on a trip; no issues with competing over clothes and style – bullying is avoided
    Against: can be expensive; students are all the same – lack of individuality; students are not relaxed – so not working well; too rigid; many countries and some schools in the UK don't require uniform; can be uncomfortable; can cause external bullying with rival schools

Unit 25

1   Positive: outstanding, clever, believable, dramatic, exciting
    Negative: obscure, lengthy, slow, verbose, predictable, incomprehensible
3   Paragraph 1: indication of narrator and main themes and general events in the plot
    Paragraph 2: related to other books by same author, style of writing, emotional impact, reviewer's opinion
4   'beautifully written'; 'clear prose'; 'pull at your heartstrings'; 'entertaining and apt'; 'timeless'; 'modern classic'
5   'even the most hardened teenager'

Glossary

act a division of a play, rather like a chapter in a book

adjective a describing word that tells us more about a noun or pronoun (e.g. The house was *spooky*; it was *huge*.)

alliteration repetition of a consonant sound at the beginnings of words (e.g. *b*ig *b*ubble)

audience the people watching a play or a television programme, or reading a book; also the people at whom an advertisement is aimed

autobiography someone's life story written by that person

ballad a narrative poem written in quatrains (four-line stanzas), often with a refrain (repeated lines)

bias supporting one side, or one opinion, more than another. Writing can be deliberately or accidentally biased.

campaign in advertising, the promotion of a product using marketing and advertising

climax the peak moment or highlight of a story or play

colloquial ordinary, everyday (speech). 'Fancy a bite to eat?' is colloquial. 'Would you like something to eat?' is not.

complication the moment in a play or story when a problem is first introduced

dialect a style of English used in one area, or in other English-speaking countries. Dialects differ from Standard English in grammar (e.g. word order) and vocabulary (actual words used; e.g. 'grockle', a West Country word for a tourist).

dialogue conversation in a novel, story or a play

drafting preparing earlier versions of a piece of writing before the final product

emotive language language used to stir up the reader's emotions (e.g. The mechanical diggers *gouged a deep wound* in the green hillside.)

fact a piece of information which can be proven and is generally agreed to be true

fiction made-up stories

form the category into which a piece of writing falls (e.g. a leaflet, a play, a novel); in poetry, the shape a poem takes

formality the level of seriousness in the style of language, usually depending on the situation; for example, you would use formal language in an interview

genre type of literature or film (e.g. horror)

grammar the rules by which we order and combine different types of words in sentences

haiku a Japanese poem of 17 syllables, in three lines of 5, 7 and 5

image a word picture used to make an idea come alive (e.g. a metaphor or simile)

imagery language that uses word pictures to make ideas come alive

irony use of words to convey the opposite of their literal meaning

jargon specialised language of a particular group (e.g. 'thrombosis' is medical jargon)

legend an old story, usually involving good and evil, gods, heroes and heroines; originally based on real events

logo symbol or emblem associated with a product or brand

metaphor a comparison of two things where one is said to be the other or act like the other (e.g. He *hammered* the ball into the open goal.)

metre in poetry, a set pattern of rhythm and number of syllables in a line

mini saga a story told in 50 words

mood the emotion conveyed to the reader by a piece of writing

myth an old story, usually involving gods and humankind, which has been passed down from one generation to the next and developed on the way. Myths are not historically true, but they can contain hidden meaning.

narrative story-telling

narrator a person telling a story

noun a word for a thing. This could be a thing you could touch, such as a *dog*, a *bike* or a *house*; or something abstract, such as *freedom*, *love* or *happiness*. Names of people and places are called proper nouns.

onomatopoeia the use of a word whose sound echoes its meaning (e.g. *ping-pong*; *miaow*; *thud*)

opinion a viewpoint. This differs from a fact.

parody imitation of a type of writing often for humorous effect

personification a description of something that is not alive as if it were a person (e.g. Time marches on.)

plot the storyline of a novel, story or play

pronoun a word that takes the place of a noun (e.g. he, she, it)

register the style of speech appropriate to a particular situation. This depends on who we are speaking to, what we are speaking about, and why we are speaking.

resolution the moment in a story or play when loose ends are tied up and problems are solved

review a report about a film or book that outlines plot, indicates genre and expresses opinions

rhetorical question a question that is used for effect and that does not need an answer

rhyme when two words begin with different sounds and end in the same sound (e.g. f*ish*, d*ish*)

rhythm in poetry, the pattern of speed variations that the syllables in a line force you to make as you say the line; the beat

satire a manner of writing that ridicules or pokes fun at its subject

scene a division of a play smaller than an act. In a scene, all the action is usually in one place.

setting the place in which the action of a story occurs, which usually affects the atmosphere (e.g. the wild moor where the witches meet in Shakespeare's *Macbeth*)

Shakespeare sonnet A Shakespeare sonnet has fourteen lines, divided into two sections: eight followed by six. Often the first eight pose a question that the next six lines answer. It rhymes ABABCDCD/ EFEFGG.

Standard English the most widely understood style of English, spoken by all those who want to be understood by strangers or the general public, such as newsreaders or politicians. It can be spoken in any accent, but cannot include dialect.

stanza a paragraph of verse in poetry

structure how a plot, text or poem is organised

syllable the smallest pronounceable part of a word (e.g. 'elephant' has three syllables)

symbol something used to represent something else (e.g. a rose might be used as a symbol of love)

tense the form of a verb which shows *when* something is happening (e.g. I *go*, I *went*, I *will go*)

theme an idea explored by an author (e.g. time, or revenge). In advertising, an idea that runs through a whole campaign.

verb a doing word (e.g. swim, laugh, run, play, remember)

vocabulary the range of words used in speech or writing